SCHOOLS FOR GROWTH

Radical Alternatives
to Current Educational Models

◆ ◆ ◆

SCHOOLS FOR GROWTH

Radical Alternatives
to Current Educational Models

◆ ◆ ◆

Lois Holzman
*East Side Institute for Short Term Psychotherapy,
New York*

IEA LAWRENCE ERLBAUM ASSOCIATES, PUBLISHERS
1997 Mahwah, New Jersey   London

Lawrence Erlbaum Associates, Inc., Publishers
10 Industrial Avenue
Mahwah, New Jersey 07430

Library of Congress Cataloging-in-Publication Data

Holzman, Lois
    Schools for growth : radical alternatives to current educational
models / Lois Holzman.
        p.   cm.
    Includes bibliographical references (p.) and index.
    ISBN 0-8058-2356-5 (cloth : alk. paper). — ISBN 0-8058-2357-3
(paper : alk. paper)
        1. Alternative schools—United States—Case studies.
    2. Alternative education—United States—Case studies.
    3. Developmental psychology—United States—Case studies.
    4. Learning, Psychology of—Case studies. I. Title.
    LC46.4.H65 1997
    371.04—dc21   97-13494
                                                             CIP

Books published by Lawrence Erlbaum Associates are printed
on acid-free paper, and their bindings are chosen for strength
and durability.

Printed in the United States of America
10 9 8 7 6 5 4 3 2 1

Contents

◆ ◆ ◆

Preface   ix

PART I: CURRENT EDUCATIONAL MODELS: MISGUIDED BY SCIENTIFIC PSYCHOLOGY

Chapter 1   *Can Schools Be Growthful in a Nongrowthful*   5
                World?

Chapter 2   *Development and Learning: What Psychology Has*   20
                Constructed

PART II: A NEW CULTURAL, PERFORMATORY PSYCHOLOGY

Chapter 3   *Vygotsky's Promise: The Unity*   51
                Learning–Leading–Development

Chapter 4   *Performing Development: Nonepistemological*   64
                Learning

**PART III: RADICAL EDUCATIONAL ALTERNATIVES
AND THEIR DEVELOPMENTAL POTENTIAL**

Chapter 5   *Project Golden Key: A Russian Experiment*   83
                 in Developmental Education

Chapter 6   *When Democratic Education*   93
                 Is Developmental: The Sudbury Valley
                 School Model

Chapter 7   *The Barbara Taylor School: A Development*   107
                 Community Where Children Learn

Chapter 8   *Not a Conclusion*   127

                 References   130

                 Author Index   139

                 Subject Index   143

To the young people of the All Stars Talent Show Network—who create hope and possibility each day as they build environments in which they can grow in a deadly and violent world

◆ ◆ ◆

Preface

◆ ◆ ◆

Schools for growth—ones where developmental learning occurs—are much more like theatrical stages than classrooms. This is my thesis. *Schools for Growth* "unpacks" this claim in several ways: by examining how psychology's conceptions of development and learning actually thwart development and learning; by offering a radically new cultural and performatory psychology based on a revolutionary reading of Lev Vygotsky and many years of independent community-building practice; and by examining a few radical educational models that are not grounded in the conceptions and investigative practices of the dominant psychology.

Exploring education's psychological and philosophical roots, we find Western culture's obsession with knowledge (cognition, epistemology) perpetuated in educational theory and practice that overidentifies learning with knowing. I argue that as long as schools continue to try to produce "knowers" (children who know how to read, count, write, be nice to each other, not fight, think critically, and so on), they will not only fail in this task, but also thwart the kind of creative, continuously emergent developmental activity that characterizes infancy and early childhood. For it is in activating the human capacity to perform—to create ourselves by being who we are not— and to collectively create performatory environments that we learn and develop.

Schools for Growth was written with both the novice and the specialist in mind. Hopefully, both will find things that require "performing beyond themselves" (to use Vygotsky's phrase). Some of the discussion of developmental theory and philosophy (especially dialectics and activity theory) might be hard going for those unfamiliar with the terminology. The school practices described in Part III concretize much of this earlier theoretical discussion, so the reader might want to flip back and forth. I have tried to create a book that deconstructs the philosophical presuppositions of developmental and learning theory in order to help teachers, teachers-in-training, teacher educators, researchers, and perhaps, parents see the extent to which our assumptions constrain and confine us and our children. Equally important—and, I hope, provocative in the most growthful sense of the word—are the wonderfully different performatory and democratic educational projects I present.

ACKNOWLEDGMENTS

This book owes its life to the committed and creative educators who have been so giving to me and have allowed me to give to them. My thanks to:

Barbara Taylor, for the privilege of working with her to shape a developmental learning approach and the school that bears her name, and to the school's children, learning directors, interns, and parents with whom we learned—sometimes joyously and sometimes painfully—but always developmentally;

Gita Vygodskaya for her warmth, insight, and support, and for introducing me to the rest of her family;

Elena Kravtsova and Gennady Kravtsov, for generously sharing their marvelous Russian educational project, Golden Key, with me;

Dan and Hanna Greenberg for the wealth of information, experience, and enthusiasm their 25-year labor of love—the Sudbury Valley School—has produced; and

Elena Lampert Schepel and Boris Gindis, two Russian-American friends and colleagues who gave their translation skills, knowledge of Vygotsky, and much more.

I am grateful for all the cheerful and quality assistance I have had in the book's production process, especially the valuable research assistance of Leanne Kumin and Dana Fusco and the editing, copyediting, and word processing savvy of Phyllis Goldberg, Warren Liebesman, and Kim Svoboda.

I appreciate receiving permission to modify portions of previously and/or concurrently published works from two publishers: Routledge, for sections of *The End of Knowing: A New Developmental Way of Learning,* by Fred Newman and myself (1997); and the Greenwood Publishing Group, Inc., for a section of *Unscientific Psychology: A Cultural-Performatory Approach to Understanding Human Life,* also by Newman and Holzman (1996, Praeger, an imprint of Greenwood Publishing Group, Inc.).

I greatly appreciate the enthusiastic response by Empire State College students to my invitations to perform and philosophize with me in the college classroom. Their collaboration played an important role in the emergence of my views on learning.

I thank the Community Literacy Research Project and its contributors for financial support that made it possible for me to present this work to international audiences of psychologists and educators.

Naomi Silverman, my editor at Lawrence Erlbaum Associates, and three reviewers of the initial draft of this book—Steven Gelb, University of San Diego; Kathy Farber, Bowling Green State University; and Bill Armaline, University of Toledo—offered creative suggestions for revisions that helped shape the book's focus and, hopefully, its readability.

Fred Newman, my long-time mentor, collaborator, and intellectual playmate with whom I have learned to philosophize, was with me every step of the way—as always, relating to me beyond myself. Our co-authored works provide the basis for many of the formulations in this book, and our joint activity (with hundreds of others) creating community far exceeds any dreams I had as a young scholar.

Finally, I want to thank those whose friendship helped make this project so much fun: Mary Fridley and Jan Wootten who eagerly listened to drafts read aloud and kept checking in with me, and Dan Friedman for making every day delightful.

—*Lois Holzman*

Part I

Current Educational Models: Misguided by Scientific Psychology

◆ ◆ ◆

School taught me to be a leader instead of a bully.

*School offered me an abuse-free environment where adults
understood children and could relate to them.*

I learned what it means to work together.

I found I only had to compete with myself, and me and my family gained support.

School taught me how to be giving.

These comments of former students and graduates of a New York City alternative elementary school capture some interesting things about everyday life experience in contemporary culture. These young people are speaking of the struggle to grow in a frequently nongrowthful environment—a culture in which abuse has been normalized to the point of often passing unnoticed, support for family members is rare, and many children and adults see their choice as limited to being a bully or being bullied. Their words strike me (to use current parlance) as more postmodern than modern. They are process- rather than product-oriented, relational and activistic rather than truth-referential or knowledge-based. Such characteristics speak to what I mean by *schools for growth* and their key elements, *developmental activity* and *developmental learning*.

More and more psychologists—myself included—are casting a critical eye at developmental theory and research and finding them ideologically biased and methodologically flawed.[1] According to the dominant psychology, human development is purported to have the following characteristics: it happens *to* individuals; it is an evolutionary, hierarchical, and essentially internal process; it evolves in a sequence of stages; it encompasses the emergence of the individuated self and the formation of identity through the interplay of attachment and separation; and it is neatly and meaningfully divisible into cognitive, physical, emotional, social, and other component parts. Maybe we have gotten it wrong all these years, some of us think. Maybe this model of human development, based on Western modes of thought (ancient philosophy and modern science), retains their dualistic presuppositions, especially the presupposition of an inner world and an outer reality. Maybe human beings are of such a qualitatively different nature from everything else that the methods of inquiry useful for the analysis of physical phenomena are inappropriate for the study of the human–social realm. Maybe development is mere ideology—a socially constructed myth and pseudoscientific term rather than something that actually occurs.

Alternatively, perhaps development is real enough—not as something that happens in or to the individual, but as ongoing, continuously emergent, social–cultural, relational activity that people themselves create. Perhaps we have unwittingly been confusing the map (development according to psychology) with what it supposedly maps (the life activity of human beings). Delineating the problems with psychology's conception of human development and attempting to formulate a relational, activistic alternative is, in my view, one of the most potent of the current challenges posed to the paradigm of scientific psychology by critical and postmodern approaches. In chapters 1 and 2, I use these sources to examine the history and methodology of psychology's construction of development, learning, childhood, and other conceptions relevant to the role and functions of schooling. Of equal importance, I feel, is to socially situate the ideas put forth in this book and present the history of their production. Toward this end, I describe my particular social–cultural–political location ("where I am coming from," if you will).

It is my view that the modern conception of development is antidevelopmental and significantly contributes to arresting developmental activity and to educational failure. Furthermore, as learning theory (so-called) has become infused with developmental theory (so-called) over the past 30 years, the overly cognitive manner in which psychologists have come to think about thinking, learning, and development has become more perva-

---

[1]Problems with developmental theory are discussed extensively in chapter 2. In addition to the critical texts I draw on there (Burman, 1994; Morss, 1990, 1993, 1995), the journal *Theory & Psychology* is a source of contemporary dialogue, especially a special issue guest edited by Bradley and Kessen (1993). See also the earlier works of Broughton (1987); Bulhan (1985); Gilligan (1982); and Henriques, Holloway, Urwin, Venn, and Walkerdine (1984).

sive in education. Ironically, the more developmental psychology has come to influence education, the less development (i.e., developmental activity) is a concern of either educational theory or school practice. This, I argue, is because developmental theory—in its failure to recognize the human capacity for relational, revolutionary activity—is antidevelopment.

Part II, "A New Cultural, Performatory Psychology," puts forth a so-cial–constructionist, activity–theoretic conception of development. This view, and the practices associated with it, are an alternative to the concep-tion that scientific psychology has constructed. I present evidence for understanding how human beings develop in terms of relational, revolution-ary activity, first focusing on the debt this approach owes to the work of Lev Vygotsky, the Soviet psychologist/methodologist of the 1920s and 1930s. I then discuss in more detail the methodological foundation of the social practice I call *developmental learning*. Its history of production over the past 25 years includes the transformation and synthesis of the work of Vygotsky and the 20th century philosopher Ludwig Wittgenstein into a nonepistemological and performatory therapeutic and educational practice.

Part III, "Radical Educational Alternatives and Their Developmental Potential," presents educational projects that are self-conscious attempts to break with key elements of modern epistemology and the dominant psycho-logical paradigm as they are perpetuated in contemporary educational theory and practice. The three projects I examine in some detail differ from each other in orientation and philosophy. The child centers that follow the approach of the Golden Key project make a sharp break with the tradition of Russian schooling. Strongly influenced by Vygotsky, they have created a pedagogy based on the belief that learning and development are first and foremost cultural phenomena. They are organized to maximize the devel-opmental benefits of certain key features of the culture of the family, particularly the support it provides for very young children to engage in developmental learning activities. The Sudbury Valley School in Massachu-setts (and its offshoots in the United States and abroad) are based on a libertarian philosophy. These schools have abandoned curriculum and teaching altogether, believing that they stifle the human spirit and are, moreover, anachronistic in a postindustrial world. Finally, the Barbara Taylor School is representative of the nonepistemological, therapeutic, and performatory methodology with which I have been involved.

Each of these schools, I argue, is more development-centered than learning/knowing-centered. Their specific philosophies and practices high-light important methodological issues that are raised in the attempt to create "postmodern" schools—schools more concerned with growing than with knowing—in cultures and societies in which the modern epistemological paradigm is so strongly entrenched and knowing is so highly valued.

The way I formulate the educational dilemma we currently face is, of course, a function of who I am—a developmentalist. I hope it is not wholly idiosyncratic, but resonates with others and is reminiscent of other formulations. As I see it, the difficult questions before us are these: Can we create ways for people to learn the kinds of things that are necessary for functional adaptation without stifling their capacity to continuously create their growth? Can schools become environments that support children to perform not only as learners but as developers of their lives? The prevalent mode of education—acquisitional learning—is grounded in a world view and a psychology which give primacy to knowing. This is, in my view, inconsistent with ongoing developmental activity. Can we create developmental learning and schools for growth?

This book is both about discovering (developing) development and a continuation of my own journey to discover it/to develop. It attempts to deconstruct the existing relationship between development, learning, and schooling and to reconstruct a new relationship centered in developmental activity. It presents concrete practices from specific educational programs operating in the United States and elsewhere that focus on the *activity of developing*, rather than on adaptation and learning (or even development) as usually understood. The new perspective on development is offered in the hope that it might contribute to creating the sort of environment in which all varieties of new ideas and educational innovations can be seen, heard, enthusiastically supported, and continue to develop.

Chapter 1

Can Schools Be Growthful in a Nongrowthful World?

◆ ◆ ◆

A few years ago, a high-level bureaucrat—the director of a major department within the New York City Board of Education—spent a few hours at the Barbara Taylor School, a small, independent, laboratory elementary school in New York City where I was the director. He said to me and to Barbara Taylor, the founder and principal, "What you're doing is a miracle." We never heard from nor saw him again.

Now, I happen not to believe in miracles (and I have no idea whether this man does or not). But those few words and his subsequent silence speak volumes. For me, they capture the dilemma of this country's current educational crisis: what are essentially structural problems are treated with symptomological solutions. I am not referring here to organizational and managerial structure, but to what we might call the *philosophical* structure of education—the core assumptions and presuppositions that underlie how schooling is done. These include the family of conceptions associated with education, such as learning and learners, teaching and teachers, knowing, knowledge, and knowers.

In what follows, I argue that an epistemological paradigm—a model of human understanding that is based on knowledge, that is, on knowing x about y—is education's chief structural defect. Like other societal institutions in Western culture, schools are committed to the philosophical position that human life and growth require some way of knowing the world. This belief, thousands of years old, has rarely been challenged; indeed, it is taken to be as "natural" as our upright stance. Whereas many contemporary scientists, social scientists, educators, social theorists, and critics argue against *modern epistemology* with its insistence on objective knowledge and Truth (with a capital T), and call for an alternative epistemology (such as a social epistemology, or "woman's ways of knowing"), almost no one suggests

5

that we attempt to give up or get rid of epistemology altogether. It is this possibility—and its implications for schooling—that I consider.

In my opinion, we need to question whether *knowing* itself—not merely the kind of ideologically biased knowing that schools perpetuate—is the source of our problems. Might it be that centuries-old philosophical biases about what it means to understand, to mean, to learn—to be human—have as much to do with how schools run as do politics, economics, and pedagogy? Might it be that the overidentification of learning and teaching with the production, dissemination, and construction of knowledge is at the root of school failure, teacher discontent, and school mismanagement? Might we not need to consider the possibility that "knowing" has run its historical course? Might it be possible that we human beings *no longer need to know* and, further, that continuing to employ knowing (cognition, an epistemological paradigm) when it has outlived its usefulness is potentially destructive of human life? In my view, without considering these questions as part of a re-examination of the philosophical structure of education, we will continue to treat only symptoms.

The circumstances of history seem to raise such unsettling questions. What many theorists today call postmodernism refers to both the circumstances that give rise to these kinds of questions and the questions themselves. Modernism (some call it modernity)—the historical period during which modern science and technology, industrialization, the discovery of the real, the ideas of progress and enlightenment, and so on—has ended, we are told. Postmodernism (or postmodernity) typically is characterized as a breakdown of categories, truth, objectivity, and meaning. If there is anything is to be discovered, we are told, it is that there is no reality, that there is nothing more to be discovered. Although a review of the voluminous postmodern literature is beyond the scope of the present book, I occasionally make reference to some current postmodern writings.[1]

Regardless of whether one views postmodernism as an accurate characterization of the current historical period, the latest "buzz word" of intellectuals, or somewhere in between, something unsettling at the core of our daily existence *is* going on in the world. Even within the natural and physical sciences, there are many who suggest that we have reached the limits of knowledge (Horgan, 1996). Certainly, those of us who deal with the human–social realm need to raise this question too; the quantity and intensity of social–psychological problems we currently face demand such an inquiry. The educational crisis requires, it seems to me, more than a critique of scientific knowing or a reform of traditional ways of knowing, learning, and teaching. It requires investigating the presuppositions of the grand narrative

---

[1]For accessible discussions of and/or by leading postmodern thinkers, see Best and Kellner (1991), Gergen (1982, 1991, 1994), Kvale (1992), Lyotard (1984), Peters (1995), and Readings (1996).

of "a knowing mind" confronting, discovering, or even constructing the world.

Within the educational research literature, these foundational philosophical issues have, by and large, been neglected in favor of research that treats the symptoms—the students who fail to learn, the teachers who fail to teach, the schools that fail to educate, the curricula that discriminate and distort, the tests and measurements that paint incomplete or false pictures. How else can we account for the systematic and conscious ignoring of those educational practices (the Barbara Taylor School being just one among thousands of learning alternatives) that radically challenge these structural presumptions of conventional schooling? How else can we understand the negligible impact of well-funded and highly publicized reform efforts that do *not* pose a thoroughgoing structural challenge? Far from saying such work should not be done, I am arguing that its impact will remain negligible without directly addressing the structural philosophical presumptions of schooling.

As a developmental psychologist and "radical" educator, I travel in and around many circles, including the "alternative schools movement," the cultural historical activity theory grouping inspired by Lev Vygotsky, and the social constructionist and deconstructionist movements within postmodernism. I have visited alternative schools in several countries, am familiar with conventional schools, and have spoken with enough educational reformers to know that they are, by and large, sincere people with good intentions. I am frequently told by a colleague, student, or parent about a wonderful school or classroom. Or I find a newspaper article, research report, or book describing a radically innovative and highly successful education project. As I listen or read, I think of the millions of parents, teachers, and students whose lives will not be touched by this work. I think of how few Americans know about the existence (let alone the practices) of the 6,000 educational alternatives in this country that have been compiled in *The Almanac of Education Choices* (Mintz, 1995). I think of the many educational experts who dismiss, in simplistic and knee-jerk fashion, the rapid growth in homeschooling as a reactionary move against public education.[2] I think of that visitor from the Board of Education.

CREATING COMMUNITY

I come from and have been shaped by an intellectual tradition of challenging existing paradigms. As a graduate student in developmental psychology at Teachers College, Columbia University in the early 1970s, I worked closely

---

[2]A recent article in the *APA Monitor* on psychologists' concerns with the effects of homeschooling on children reported that from 1990 to 1996, the number of children schooled at home tripled—from 300,000 to 900,000 (Murray, 1996, p. 1).

with Lois Bloom on her pioneering studies of children's early language.[3] Bloom was charting new ground then, one of a handful of researchers around the country who were looking outside developmental psychology proper for tools with which to create a new research methodology. (Now standard fare within language acquisition research, 25 years ago this was rather controversial.) The longitudinal and observational approach we developed—spending time with young children in their homes over an extended period of time, taping our conversations, and noting what activities we and the children were engaged in—was influenced more by ethnography and linguistics than by psychology. So was our method of data analysis—letting the categories "emerge from the data" as opposed to imposing predetermined ones. I recall that this bothered some people; they refused to take the work seriously because, they said, it did not meet the strict criteria of the accepted scientific paradigm. I think, however, that those who got riled up did so because creating new methods of investigation calls into question the very nature of the thing you are investigating. In this case, our work was initially threatening (and ignored) to the extent that it challenged the accepted conception of language and language behavior.

I left Columbia and Bloom in 1976, PhD dissertation completed. I moved across town and downtown to the Rockefeller University, having the good fortune again to work with a maverick. Michael Cole (who is now a leading proponent of cultural historical psychology) had set up the Laboratory of Comparative Human Cognition there with major foundation support. I was part of a research team that pioneered what was, at the time, new technology and a new methodology for investigating learning, literacy, and schooling as cultural phenomena. Concerned with inequality, we saw schools as both perpetuators of class, race, and gender bias and potential forces for transforming such bias. We believed that the dominant psychological paradigm—its view of what a person is, what learning and development and culture are—played a significant role in allowing certain children to succeed in school and others to fail. We hoped we could make some discoveries and create something psychologically and perhaps pedagogically useful. In this effort, Soviet psychology—in particular the writings of Vygotsky and work carried on by his followers—was especially valuable.

Again, the creative effort to develop a new research approach exposed some core assumptions of the dominant psychological paradigm. In this case, we became convinced that the psychological laboratory was more than a physical space—it was a methodology that systematically excluded critical features of human activity, for example, how people learn, think, and solve

---

[3]These studies include Bloom (1970, 1973) and a series of articles and chapters done collaboratively during the 1970s and 1980s. Many of these have been collected in the volume *Language Development from Two to Three* (Bloom, 1991). During these years, I published under the name Lois Hood.

problems. We documented as precisely as we could how cognitive processes are socially constructed, and concluded that experimental, cognitive psychology was *ecologically invalid*. We wrote an honest, provocative, and well-researched monograph (Cole, Hood, & McDermott, 1978) and sent it off to a leading psychology journal with a reputation for publishing works of potential theoretical significance.

The monograph was rejected out of hand for not being scientific. I remember thinking, "That's the very point we're making—we're arguing that the criteria of science are invalid—so how can that be a reason for rejection?" But, what really surprised me was the lack of interest in our work displayed by such respected scientists. They essentially ignored us, neither arguing against, agreeing with, nor critiquing anything substantive in what we had presented. They seemed more annoyed than anything else that we were trying to break new ground.

The Rockefeller University began phasing out its support for psychology in the late 1970s (its philosophy programs had already fallen by the wayside). Cole accepted an offer from the University of California at San Diego and moved the Laboratory there in 1979. Not wanting to leave New York City, I joined the faculty of Empire State College, State University of New York— then an 8-year-old experiment in nontraditional undergraduate education—as a "mentor" in human development and educational studies. Again, I had found a niche within—albeit on the edges of—the mainstream. And, once again, I was working with people who were self-consciously challenging the dominant paradigm of learning, this time as practitioners.

There is always a contradiction in challenging institutional arrangements (even, or especially, as mavericks) from a location inside the very institutions that perpetuate and give legitimacy to those arrangements. For me, this contradiction is intensified because I have been "located" simultaneously both inside and outside the mainstream. During the time I was at the Rockefeller University, I also began working with a group of people who, in the late 1960s, had left the campuses and other established institutions. Guided by a belief that changing schools, health and mental health treatment, and politics has more to do with building new kinds of institutions and community organizing than with having the correct critical analysis, they began to establish free schools, communes, and community-based health clinics and therapy centers. These early projects were among the thousands of radical political–educational–therapeutic alternatives that sprang up all over the United States at that time.

The leader of these radical women and men was Fred Newman, a Stanford University-trained philosopher of science. He taught philosophy at several colleges and universities—getting fired from each one for giving A's to all his students to keep the men out of the draft during the Vietnam War—until he left academia in 1968 to engage full time in community organizing and radical politics. In the increasingly conservative environment of the late 1970s, when many radical alternatives folded or were co-opted into the mainstream, Newman and his co-workers moved toward creating independent institutions, focusing initially on electoral politics and psychotherapy. It was during this transitional time in the development of what has turned out to be, 20 years later, a unique synthesis of politics and psychology—*a developing development community*—that I met Newman. I was particularly impressed by the passion and respect he had for both intellectual work and the tedious process of organization-building.

A handful of us—myself, Newman, two social workers, a graduate student in sociology, a mental health researcher, and two lay therapists—founded the New York Institute for Social Therapy and Research in 1978. We all had paying day jobs; we built this therapy, education, and research center in the evenings and on weekends. The Institute offered social therapy (the clinical approach Newman was developing), classes, lectures, and a speaker series on progressive approaches to politics, psychology, education, health, and culture. As the director of research, I planned courses, taught many of them, designed community research projects, and networked with other researchers and academics. With much excitement, I "brought" Lev Vygotsky from Rockefeller University to the Institute.

At first, I saw what we were doing at the Institute and at the Rockefeller University Lab as "the same thing." Both were concerned with the same issues—for example, racism, sexism, classism, and the conservatism of the institutions of education and psychology. Both shared a commitment to making the world a better place. Both groups desired to create a new, more humane psychological and educational theory and practice. The members of both even read much of the same literature and talked about things similarly. Before too long, however, I came to realize that, despite these similarities, our activities were qualitatively different.

At the Institute and its affiliated organizations, we were attempting to create new kinds of institutions and activities that were not, at the outset, overdetermined by the constraints and conventions of traditional institutions. Our desire was to create some sort of activity that was inclusive, radically democratic, and potentially developmental. As we saw it then and still do, financial independence is essential for creating the kinds of environments we sought. For it was not only the obvious strings attached to money or institutional affiliation that concerned us (such as making the funding source or institution look good and/or finding the results they desired). We were equally committed to creating environments in which the traditional knowledge-seeking and knowledge-producing paradigm (complete with concepts such as proof, hypothesis testing, objectivity, results, and evaluation) and its accompanying institutional arrangements (such as boundaries, categories, definitions, rules, and regulations) are not built in.

The fact that we survived and our work continued to grow owes much to our neither being affiliated with any university nor funded by corporate donations, foundation grants, or government subsidies. It is one thing to run an afterschool program to help young people develop alternatives to violence through the receipt of a government or foundation grant, or when the work is done under the pressure to "publish or perish" and for the purpose of getting tenure. It is quite another activity when the project's history does not include such contractual relationships with the state. As another example, building a psychotherapeutic practice that "serves" poor people is one activity when its existence depends on government funding and legislative mandates, thus requiring the use of diagnosis. It is a different activity when the practice does not label and when poor and middle-class people are in therapy together by virtue of people with more money choosing to subsidize the participation of people with less money because they believe it is psychologically helpful and/or politically important.

This kind of financial and institutional independence, of course, was no guarantee that what we would create would differ qualitatively from existing arrangements. It merely created the possibility for a new kind of institution, what we call an anti-institution (Holzman & Newman, 1979; Newman & Holzman, 1996, 1997). In the early 1980s, our understanding of human activity as the simultaneous creation of environments *and* the "products" of these environments, as well as the roots of this conception in the writings of Vygotsky and the early works of Marx (Marx & Engels, 1973; Vygotsky, 1978, 1987, 1993) were beginning to emerge. We believed that environments quickly come to overdetermine activity—*unless they are created along with the activity.*

As we understand it, the practice of independence is an organizing activity. It involves reaching out to people from all class and ethnic backgrounds in all neighborhoods and walks of life and giving them the opportunity to participate in whatever ways they choose in the work of creating new kinds of schools, medical care, political organizations, psychotherapeutic practice, and culture that meet their needs as they define them. To the extent that we have not replicated traditional institutional arrangements it is a consequence of our self-conscious attempt to create continuously emergent community. Rather than *applying* a particular fixed method, we work to *practice method*, an explicitly participatory activity that "entails the continuous, self-conscious deconstruction of the hierarchical arrangements of learning, teaching and knowing ... confronting biases, definitions, and judgments in an ongoing way ... [and] self-criticism from the perspective of the positive continuation of the developmental environment, not merely from the negative perspective of responding to imposed societal values and norms" (Holzman, 1995c, p. 24). In other words, our commitment was not simply to negate or escape from existing structures, systems, or ideas but to build something (an environment, a community) as free as possible of the assumptions of existing systems.

The most troublesome of these assumptions is that all human life and growth necessarily require knowledge, systemization, and some method of appraisal that is abstracted from the ongoing activity of life and growth (Newman, 1996; Newman & Holzman, 1996, 1997). We are not alone in seeing the dangers of this assumption, nor in recognizing it as the misguided attempt to adopt to the study of human–social phenomena a method developed by and for the natural and physical sciences (see Danziger, 1994; Gergen, 1982, 1994; Polkinghorne, 1983; Shotter, 1993a, 1993b). In our view, in order to create/discover something of value for all people, we will have to be deliberately "unscientific" and engage in the ongoing creation of nonepistemologically overdetermined, nonsystematic—and, thereby, potentially developmental— environments.

Obligated to no one but ourselves, our clients, students, and individuals who financially supported our work with no strings attached, nor to any particular interpretive method, we were able to alter radically what we were doing in a matter of moments. We could be inclusive and allow new people to reshape the totality of what we were doing. If we believed, as many clinicians do, that diagnosis is an impediment to helping people with emotional pain, we (unlike our colleagues at funded clinics) could refuse to diagnose. If we believed that intelligence is not measurable (as many educators do), then we could choose to neither grade nor sort students. Our effectiveness would be judged by our clients, not by any outside evaluative body.

Over the past 20 years, this developing development community and its independent institutions has grown dramatically, from one apartment complex in New York City to social therapy centers in several U.S. cities, from a handful of people to tens of thousands. Its work is now multifaceted and includes a research, training, and education center (the East Side Institute for Short Term Psychotherapy and its Center for Developmental Learning); the largest community-based cultural organization for inner-city youth in the country (the All Stars Talent Show Network); a highly respected multicultural off-off-Broadway theater (the Castillo Theatre); a small alternative press (Castillo International); a Vygotskian-influenced laboratory elementary school (the Barbara Taylor School); teen pregnancy and abuse prevention programs in preschools and public schools; and more. Significantly, it also includes a supporter base of 200,000 people who participate by giving their financial support to these ongoing projects.

This sociohistorical location is a critical factor in shaping my views of schooling, learning, and development and, further, the particular reading I give to psychological, educational, and philosophical literature. Although this point might seem obvious, the cultural–political history of one's activity and institutional location is often overlooked. If this were not the case, it is not clear why critical and self-reflexive approaches, for example, in social science and education, would have emerged. My particular sociohistorical location has some unique characteristics: it is designed to be nonepistemological and nonreformist (to what extent it succeeds is another story); its existence and the years of community-building activity that produced and continue to produce it are essential to my having something to say or write. It should not be surprising, therefore, that how I see schooling, learning, and development, what I take to be problematic in some contemporary educational and psychological research, and which leading thinkers have contributed most to my approach would differ—sometimes dramatically—from how others see these things.

Throughout this book, as I argue for and present illustrations of schools for growth (nonepistemological learning), I draw on the substantive insights and methodological breakthroughs of Lev Vygotsky and Ludwig Wittgenstein—*as seen from a community-building social location and a revolutionary vantage point*. The early philosophical writings of Karl Marx have also played a major role in the practice and formulations of the developing development community and my views on education. I take the three of them to be revolutionary in their attempt to create new methodologies for approaching human life as lived. This reading, like this location and vantage point, differs from that of many followers of Vygotsky and Wittgenstein (and Marx), and I will take care to point out these differences as we go along. Vygotsky is transformed in this environment from a cognitive psychologist and mediation theorist to a practicing methodologist and revolutionary scientist. Wittgenstein is transformed from an ordinary language philosopher into a therapist who helps make our problems vanish. Marx, too, is transformed from one who "spoke the Truth" into a revolutionary methodologist whose dialectical–historical materialism is practically and developmentally useful.

During the past few years, Newman and I have attempted to articulate the developmental practice of the community we have helped to build, its methodological underpinnings in the works of Vygotsky, Wittgenstein, and Marx, and its interface with contemporary intellectual movements. *Lev Vygotsky: Revolutionary Scientist* (Newman & Holzman, 1993) is primarily a theoretical discussion of Vygotsky's contribution to creating the kind of revolutionary science activity needed to reinitiate human development. *Unscientific Psychology: A Cultural–Performatory Approach to Understanding Human Life* (Newman & Holzman, 1996) expanded that discussion, locating both Wittgenstein and Vygotsky as "pre-postmodernists" who bridge the gap between modernist scientific psychology and the possibilities presented in its current postmodernization. *The End of Knowing: A New Developmental Way of Learning* (Newman & Holzman, 1997) assesses postmodern psychological and philosophical theorizing, arguing that its practicality in dealing with social policy issues lies in going beyond its current critical and reformist posture to nonepistemological, performed activity.

Schools for Growth, based on the same methodology as these other works, is about schooling and the institutionalization of learning. It presents the practicality and developmental potential of this nonepistemological approach in the area of education. For it is as a key player in the ongoing activity of creating a developing development community that I have been able to see more clearly the structural limitations of traditional educational institutions. I think it is very difficult, perhaps impossible, to see them from a location entirely inside them. As worthwhile and groundbreaking as the research work of the Laboratory of Comparative Human Cognition was, its limitations were structurally present by virtue of its being part of the educational and scientific systems that, ultimately, determine how and to what extent its members can challenge orthodox social science. As nontraditional as Empire State College was (and is), it too can only go so far in establishing an educational environment that rejects the epistemological paradigm that determines how higher learning is conducted. Societal institutions—their history and relationships—not only constrain the answers you might develop to pressing social and scientific issues; they overdetermine the very questions you ask, because they overdetermine how and what you are able to see.

In that unpublished 1978 monograph, *Ecological Niche-picking: Ecological Invalidity as an Axiom of Experimental, Cognitive Psychology*, Cole, McDermott, and I explored the question, "How come kids who are 'street smart' are 'school dumb'?" In our 1993 book, *Lev Vygotsky: Revolutionary Scientist*, Fred Newman and I repeatedly raised the question, "What are revolutionary psychologists to do?" If there is a "burning question" that played a role in the writing of *Schools for Growth*, it is this: Is there anything teachers can do in nondevelopmental environments?

For in my view, the current educational crisis is a crisis in development. Not only traditional schooling, but most efforts to reform the educational system suffer from a misidentification of the problem (and the related misidentification of the human activity of developing with what psychology calls development). Certain kids will always be "school dumb" as long as what it means to be "school smart"—to learn, to know, to understand—is not challenged at its ontological roots. In my opinion, if we simply go on relating to the crisis in learning *as an issue of learning*, if we continue to frame discussions and offer solutions within an essentially instrumental, cognitive, and individualistically based perspective, we will fail. If we do not practically and positively challenge the modern conceptions of development and of learning (and of their relationship), we will fail. What is offered in this book is a radically different perspective on schooling, one grounded in a cultural, nonscientific psychology and the conception of *developmental activity*. Creating developmental learning environments is the specific developmental activity necessary to create schools for growth. Learning, in this practice, is nothing more nor less than discovering-and-developing development. It has, I argue, relatively little to do with knowing and is a nonepistemological, performed activity.

WHY DEVELOPMENT?

Why should we be so concerned with development, you might already be asking, in a book about schooling? Shouldn't learning, the primary activity of schools, be our topic? Well, yes and no. It all depends on the overall framework from which the question is posed. Within the Vygotskian frame-work used here, a concern with development is simultaneously a concern with learning. For Vygotsky, learning and development, as social–cultural, relational activities, are inseparable; they are a unity in which learning is connected to and leads (dialectically, not linearly) development. Vygotsky (1978) said: "the only 'good learning' is that which is in advance of development" (p. 89). If we take him seriously (by which I mean metho-dologically), we surely must wonder if what goes on in most traditionally organized classrooms is worthy of being called *learning*.

It seems clear from standard educational practices such as testing and evaluation, grade levels, tracking, and developmentally appropriate teach-ing materials that Vygotsky's perspective is either unknown or disregarded, for *the unity learning–leading–development* is almost nowhere to be found. To the extent that development plays a role in the organization of teaching and learning, it is a stagist and static conception, often reduced to a point of measurement used to determine who is "capable" of learning what. Seventy years after Vygotsky pointed to its invalidity and laid the foundation for a new, radically humanistic psychology based on sociocultural relational ac-tivity, the belief that learning depends on something called an individual's "developmental level" still dominates. Learning (so-called) is the concern of schools, with developmental activity falling by the wayside.

The pragmatic, bureaucratized, curriculum-based, information- and skills-oriented (often oppressive and blatantly discriminatory) system of education that has been institutionalized in the United States for nearly 200 years managed, seemingly, to meet the needs of the nation (if not of all of its people) until relatively recently. In fact, it is not unreasonable to view the educational policy of the past as being made and carried out in the service of development to the extent that those who held positions of power in business and government were concerned with creating an environment in which a government, a culture, and an economy could optimally grow. If they made compromises that greatly sacrificed human freedom (including the freedom to discover), it was in the name of what they believed to be qualitatively transformative for America. And as long as the United States was growing—economically and in other ways—nondevelopmental school-ing seemed to produce enough people who were sufficiently educated to create more and more sophisticated technology, methods of production and distribution of goods, and the many other things that contributed to a continuously rising standard of living and accompanying cultural and scientific advances.

Within the context of a nation that was developing, such schooling even managed to produce significant numbers of young adults who themselves continued to grow. This is in no way meant to deny the human deprivation and destruction produced by the class, race, and gender inequalities of the United States in its "glory days." Rather, it is to highlight the transformed *total environment* of the late 20th century in which such inequalities persist. For my argument on behalf of *schools for growth* rests, in large part, on a particular understanding of the specific historical moment we find ourselves in at the dawn of the 21st century—a moment when development is grinding to a halt, and there is a growing gap between our developmental needs and our learning needs.

The evidence is strong. Statistics finally show what insightful analysts have been saying for nearly a decade: the current generation of Americans is the first in the nation's history that will not have a higher standard of living than the preceding one. The economy, for one thing, is not growing. Unlike other periods in American history when changes in the U.S. economy were felt across class lines (albeit very unequally), current economic changes at the top do not impact on America's masses; ordinary people do not reap the results. According to the U.S. Census Bureau, the income disparity between "the most affluent Americans and everyone else" was wider between 1988 and 1994 than at any time since the end of World War II (Holmes, 1996, p. A1). The economy may be expanding, but it is not developing.

There are other social, political, and cultural characteristics of contemporary life that, to me, indicate ways in which our developmental needs are not being met, much less thought about. For example, the trend toward increasing medicalization, particularly of children who are diagnosed with so-called cognitive or affective deficits, might well be an effective means of controlling symptoms. It is not, however, a particularly developmental approach to the continued growth of young children. The intensity and nature of violence (from nationalistic genocide to drive-by shootings), the myopia of policymakers who opt for pragmatic solutions to social problems, and the attitude toward homelessness and school failure—as things that will always be with us, as problems that we can, at best, reduce—are, among other things, expressive of an acceptance of nondevelopment or a disbelief in qualitative transformation of totalities.

In *Schooling the Poor*, an inquiry into the American school experience from the earliest pauper schools through contemporary public schools, Rothstein (1994) provided a chilling picture of early American schools:

Again and again, throughout the nineteenth century, the same basic principles or beliefs were repeated in different educational experiences and circumstances. The common schoolers ... and the movement toward greater uniformity in pedagogic methods assumed a correct form of language and knowledge acquisition, a superior cultural and linguistic heritage that had to be mastered. At the core of the state schooling apparatus was the feature of military discipline, a type used in mass urban institutions of every kind. A second basic feature was the enormous number of students who were labeled as failures by schools that were supposed to eliminate social inequality.... The constant call for reform that characterized the entire history of schooling and its failure to make significant inroads into the nature and character of the system made everyone aware of the change-resistant nature of the state's educational bureaucracy. Reform was part of the process that gave added legitimacy to educators and their work while changing little in the way things were actually done inside the bounded schools themselves. (p. 93)

One of the interesting things about this description of education in the 19th century is how it appears quite appropriate to our times, but in a most important way it does not fit the contemporary situation at all. The meaning of the practices Rothstein described is qualitatively different by virtue of the fact that the world in which these practices are occurring is vastly different. The immovability of educational bureaucracy, the cultural elitism of curriculum, the acquisitional model of learning, and the legitimacy given to the status quo by the discourse of educational reformers all mean something very different in a culture that is not developing economically, intellectually, socially, culturally, or morally. The kinds of decisions on educational policy being made today can no longer be justified in the name of development, economic or otherwise. Nondevelopmental schooling in a nondeveloping world is devastating. For the acquisition of skills and information, although obviously essential for societal adaptation and the continuation of a society and culture, does not lead to qualitative transformation; it is the assimilation of what already exists. Development, however, is the creating of something new. There is, apparently, no end to the information human beings are capable of producing. But without developing, our society may prove incapable of producing *learners*. This is what I mean by the growing gap between our development needs and our learning needs.

Two centuries of learning severed from development (developmental activity) and tied to knowledge acquisition and cognitive skills, to my way of thinking, has got us to this crisis point. The "chickens came home to roost," so to speak, in the 1960s. Several converging factors forced us to confront the consequences of nondevelopmental, acquisition-based learning educational practices. The evidence that education had failed to be the great equalizer could no longer be ignored. The disparity between children of color and White children relative to school access and school success was no longer simply acknowledged as a fact of life. The civil rights, anti-war, and varied liberation movements brought a recognition of and sensitivity to how schools are not merely passively ineffectual in eliminating inequality;

they actively reproduce and perpetuate it. Partially from these *identity politics*[4] struggles, then, did the important movements for critical and radical pedagogies emerge.

In addition, changes occurring in scientific psychology—in particular, the discovery/social construction/production of "the developing child" and the reintroduction of "theories of mind" through the construction of the Piagetian paradigm and cognitive psychology—breathed new life into developmental and educational psychology. Schools could be radically transformed into highly successful institutions of learning, it was believed, through the application of the discoveries of development psychology. The opportunistic use by government of both the political and intellectual/scientific protest movements can be seen in many aspects of the War on Poverty, including the marketing of *remediation* as a credible approach to resolving inequity and the launching of federally funded interventions such as Head Start.

Thirty years later, the learning crisis of American society has only increased. Although statistics cover over the manifestations of the crisis as lived day-to-day, they can, nevertheless, be helpful in highlighting the severity of the crisis. Whether or not one agrees with the Goals 2000: Educate America Act signed into law in 1994, the dismal record thus far is surely worrisome. According to the *National Education Goals Report* (1995), rather than making strides in reaching the goals, there has been a decline or no change in nearly all measures of the eight goals. For example, the report states that reading achievement at Grade 12 has declined (from 37% to 34%) and remains unchanged at Grades 4 and 8 (both below 30%); the high school completion rate is steady at 86%; the United States is still ranked last in a comparison of the mathematics achievement of 13-year-olds among five countries; and the gap between White and minority students in college enrollment and completion is unchanged.

The failure of special education provides more evidence for the way in which psychology has contributed to the worsening learning crisis. A recent *New York Times* article (Richardson, 1995) examining special education in New York City public schools reported these disconcerting facts. One in four Board of Education employees are involved in the delivery of services to special education students, who represent 13% of all New York City students (this is twice the national average). Fewer than 33% of these students are defined as handicapped; the rest are diagnosed as learning disabled (LD) or emotionally disturbed (ED). It is well known that a disproportionate number of these students who are segregated into special classes are Black or Latino boys. What happens to these children? Fewer than 5% graduate from high school in 4 years and only 25% ever receive some kind of diploma. It is

---

[4]The term *identity politics* refers to claims of rights made on the basis of group identity. See Part II.

difficult to conceive of a criterion on which to base the continuation of so costly a project with such disastrous results. In the opinion of some psychologists and educators, special education and the syndromes that increasingly come to comprise it (e.g., LD, ED, ACHD) is one of scientific psychology's most lucrative contemporary myths that has tragic consequences for hundreds of thousands of children and their families (see Coles, 1987; Finlan, 1994; Taylor, 1991).

Schooling and learning appear to be on a collision course (Perlman, 1992). Neither remediation, special education, the insertion of psychology into education, nor the critiques made by sociologists of education have halted the failure of learning-centered, knowledge-oriented schooling. I do not think they can. For the crisis in learning is equally a crisis in development, and without addressing the extent to which schools, educational models, and the psychology on which they are based are antidevelopmental—by virtue of their adherence to epistemology and a knowing paradigm—I do not think reform efforts can succeed. In Part II I present arguments and evidence for the positive alternative of reinitiating the social–cultural–historical activity of creating developmental activity through performance. But, before this reconstruction, we need to begin deconstructing psychology's conceptions of development and learning.

Chapter 2

Development and Learning:
What Psychology Has Constructed

◆ ◆ ◆

IS DEVELOPMENTAL PSYCHOLOGY DEVELOPMENTAL?

Trained as a developmental psychologist, I learned the boundaries of the field as well as the next graduate student. Nevertheless, I found the implication unsettling: if developmental psychology is a "branch" of the psychological study of human beings, then there are aspects of human functioning and activity that are, presumably, not developmental. The distinction between developmental psychology and other branches such as personality, learning, social psychology and educational psychology seemed particularly disturbing. Years later, I learned that there had been psychologists who argued, even before the term *developmental psychology* was coined, that development is not an area of psychology at all but an approach to the investigation of human–social phenomena.[1]

As a distinct branch of psychology on a par with clinical, experimental, industrial, and educational, developmental psychology began with the child. Not only was this its subject matter until very recently; its historical roots are in the "child study" movement of the late 1800s and early 1900s.

The Construction of the Child and Childhood

Charles Darwin's 1877 text, *A Biographical Sketch of an Infant*, excerpts from notebooks of observations of his son (which he had begun recording 40 years earlier), is cited as the first child study in the received history of psychology. Not surprisingly, Darwin's interest in children was an evolutionary one. He

---

[1]A version of this discussion with a more philosophical bent appears as chapter 6, "Psychology and Human Development: The Ideal(ist) Marriage," in Newman and Holzman (1996).

wanted to find evidence that our mental and moral faculties had evolved from our animal ancestry (Morss, 1990). Early development was important to him as "the hereditary endowment, a baseline from which variation might emerge in the *adult* state" (Morss, 1990, p. 15).

This interest in children, not in their own right but as the means through which "the laws of nature" get expressed, has remained, by and large, the *raison d'etre* for developmental research over the century. Despite the fact that late 20th century biology has advanced well beyond Darwin and that our concept of childhood has changed rather dramatically, human development studies remain bound to an evolutionary framework. In the view of some critical developmental psychologists (e.g., Burman, 1994; Morss, 1990, 1995), the presumption of an evolutionary process (and its implied hierarchy) is precisely what is troublesome about developmental psychology, for this distorts the object of study.

Developmental psychology has become a major testing ground for the kinds of epistemological questions philosophers have been asking for centuries: How do we know (see, think, feel) what we know (see, think, feel)? To put it simply, but not inaccurately, developmental psychology's own epistemology— "What adults know can be discovered by discovering what babies know"—is a restatement of philosophy's fundamental presuppositions about the mind. Thousands of years of Western thinking about thinking became more deeply insinuated into Western culture when mental processes began to be investigated scientifically.

We are slightly ahead of our story, however, because in order for children to be worthy of study, they had to exist! There had to be a concept of the child and the identification of a phase of life distinct from adulthood. Childhood is thereby as much a cultural phenomenon as a biological one. In his classic *Centuries of Childhood* (1962), the French historian Philippe Ariès argues that the modern Western conception of childhood was socially constructed during the 16th and 17th centuries "at a time when the family had freed itself from both biology and law to become a value, a theme of expression, an occasion of emotion" (p. 10).

Combing diaries and examining paintings produced over a period of 400 years, Ariès claimed to have found evidence for changes in how the European aristocracy related to and talked about children and how artists of the time represented children in their paintings. He took these documents to be strongly suggestive of how children were thought about. Ariès noted, for example, that it was not until the 14th century that children began to be portrayed in paintings. Before that, in pictures where it might be expected that children would be represented (such as scenes of certain Christian religious events), they were depicted as little men. Until the 17th century, Ariès found, no ordinary children were portrayed in art; the medieval child, a holy child, or symbol of the soul, was painted nude. Ariès also quoted extensively from diaries of the time—for example, from the diary of the physician to the French king, Henri IV. These written excerpts reveal that no special treatment was accorded to children, and no special reserve was shown in their presence. Children were present in all of life's experiences, including sex, drinking, violence, and death. Ariès connected the "discovery of childhood" to various cultural and economic changes taking place in 17th-century Europe, which diminished the sociality (the public nature) of living and gave rise to the idea of the (more private) family.

From the mid-1800s through the early 1900s, views of childhood were, not surprisingly, romantic: the child was "closer" to nature than the adult, an immature biological organism, untouched by civilization, en route to knowledge and reason but lacking both (Burman, 1994). Through the early 1900s, many studies of children compared them to apes, "primitive man" or "savages," and the insane. In their observations, scientists looked for evidence of the recapitulation of certain assumed evolutionary adaptations, such as the tendency for physical and mental development to proceed from simple to complex, from homogeneous to heterogeneous, from holistic to differentiated.

The American psychologist G. Stanley Hall is typically identified as the father of developmental psychology, although he was one of the early proponents of development as an approach to, rather than a branch of, psychology. Largely forgotten today, Hall was highly influential in the first two decades of this century; it was he who put childhood and development on the psychological map. A strict believer in recapitulation, Hall supported the idea that human learning naturally followed the evolutionary course of civilization and that "education is simply the expediting and shortening of the course" (cited in Morss, 1990, p. 33). Education should therefore be "developmental"—it should take children through stages of civilization (cultural epochs) because such a curriculum would match their (recapitulatory) needs (Morss, 1990). Hall imported this model, which originated in Europe, to the United States. He also popularized the psychological census as a means of gathering data on large numbers of schoolchildren in order to gain knowledge about how mental characteristics were distributed.

Child study was soon affected by the advent of more sophisticated statistical methods and by the mental testing craze that had begun during World War I. By making "mental age" analogous to chronological age, it was now possible, so it was claimed, to see all kinds of abilities as distributed in quantifiable and measurable intervals (the familiar "milestones," such as the age at which babies hold their heads up, begin to crawl, say one word at a time, and acquire a 50-word vocabulary). Burman (1994) described how this period was critical in *naturalizing* and *normalizing* childhood as it produced the modern conception of the child. The evolutionary foundation of child study, coupled with psychology's new investigative practices of sorting, measuring, and quantifying by means of statistically aggregated data, produced knowledge claims about the supposedly natural unfolding of the human growth process. It also provided a simple baseline—age—that allowed deviations from the norm to be identified. Burman nicely summarized what many see as the ideological status of the so-called scientific conception of the child:

> The normal child, the ideal type, distilled from the comparative scores of age-graded populations, is therefore a fiction or a myth. No individual or real child lies at its basis. It is an abstraction, a fantasy, a fiction, a production of the testing apparatus that incorporates, that constructs the child, by virtue of its gaze. (pp. 16–17)

The conceptions of *natural* and *normal* are now inextricably linked with evolution (as opposed, for example, to revolution). Natural and normal are defined as continuous, steady, and linear. Things may be in a constant state of motion (a view the world has come to accept since Galileo first dared to argue it several hundred years ago), but motion and change occur at fixed intervals. Furthermore, development has been reconstituted in time; to speak of development, it now is necessary to refer to chronological age. Thus, another layer of abstraction has been established.

If what is natural and normal is *evolution*, then *revolution* necessarily becomes abnormal. In earlier works, I have argued that human development is more revolutionary than evolutionary (see especially Newman & Holzman, 1993, 1996) and that Vygotsky's insights about revolution, history, and science offered a strong challenge to an evolutionary view of development (although he was anything but consistent in this critique):

> To the naive mind, revolution and history seem incompatible. It believes that historical development continues as long as it follows a straight line. When a change comes, a break in the historical fabric, a leap—then this naive mind sees only catastrophe, a fall, a rupture; for the naive mind history ends until back again straight and narrow. The scientific mind, on the contrary, views revolution as the locomotive of history forging ahead at full speed; it regards the revolutionary epoch as a tangible, living embodiment of history. A revolution solves only those tasks which have been raised by history; this proposition holds true equally for revolution in general and for aspects of social and cultural life. (cited in Levitin, 1982, inside front cover)

Vygotsky's eloquent formulation contrasted the evolutionary perspective ("the naive mind") with a dialectical historical materialist perspective ("the scientific mind"). He urged that we take an historical (revolutionary) rather than a societal (evolutionary) view of development. His modernist language notwithstanding, his message anticipated the postmodern insistence on the historical and cultural embeddedness of knowledge and worldviews.

Vygotsky would go unheeded; indeed, his work was suppressed under Stalin and remained unknown (outside a very small circle) until the 1960s. Even if his writings had been widely available, however, it is doubtful that they would have had a significant impact. By the 1930s, biological and behaviorist reductionism (two sides of the same coin) and philosophical rationalism were already deeply ingrained in academic and research psychology. Freudian theory was transforming the cultural landscape in many ways, including how we think about the nature of children and of childhood, and it was beginning to get incorporated into psychological theorizing (Cushman, 1995; Torrey, 1992).

During this period, the dominant psychological conception of the child was as an essentially passive organism capable of being trained, molded, and socialized. The emerging popular conception of the child was more explicitly moral and conflicted, but no less passive and static. Whereas one or another image might have dominated for a brief period of time, the modern child was at once naturally good and naturally sinful, innocent and untrustworthy, dependent on "the other" and ever vulnerable to the dangers of "the outer," in need of freedom and in need of control. In the social construction of the child, the popular and scientific conceptions mutually influence each other, of course, and both are also influenced by (and influence) political, economic, and cultural transformations.

One historically important and illustrative example is the turn of the century transformation in the form of life that was urban industrialization, the concomitant rise in the standard of living, and the political activism that was a response to economic exploitation. Prior to the 20th century, children were primarily of economic value, to their families and to the larger society. Their life activity (except among the aristocracy) was work—in preindustrial times, on the land; with the industrial revolution, in the mines and factories. The successful mass movement to abolish the abhorrent conditions of child labor in Western Europe and the United States in the late 1800s created the possibility of a new way of conceptualizing children. So did the economic progress that accompanied industrialization, and the steady rise in the standard of living. So did advances in medicine and public health, which significantly lowered the rate of infant mortality.

Viviana Zelizer (1985) presented a sociological analysis of this transformative period in the United States and its impact on the construction of the child. Between the 1870s and the 1930s, Zelizer argued in *Pricing the Priceless Child*, the economic and sentimental value of children under 15 years of age reversed themselves in importance, both to parents and in the culture at large. A century ago, children were necessary sources of income (for the working class, they remained so into the 1930s). For example, to the extent that parents were compensated for the wrongful death of a child, the amount depended on the child's earning capacity. By contrast, today it costs hundreds of thousands of dollars to rear a child, who produces no income. Adoptive parents now pay tens of thousands of dollars simply to have a child to rear. Courts routinely award upwards of a million dollars for the wrongful death of a child, their decisions based on the grief, sorrow, and emotional loss sustained by the parents. The value of children is no longer economic, but sentimental.

Zelizer (1985) attributed this radical transformation in part to the increased commercialism of the society; children came to occupy a separate, *extracommercial* place: "the expulsion of children from the 'cash nexus' … was … part of a cultural process of 'sacralization' of children's lives. The term sacralization is used in the sense of objects being invested with sentimental or religious meaning" (p. 11).

Zelizer provided fascinating data to show how the construction of the "economically worthless" and "sentimentally priceless" child was effected. Her data are disconcerting; they are taken from real-life situations that are either no longer relevant or have been resolved in ways that are today taken for granted. Having to do with the life and death of children, they are situations in which the economic worth of a child and sentimental value intersect: the public response to children being killed by streetcars and automobiles; the struggle over child labor legislation; the insuring of children's lives; parental compensation for the wrongful death of children; and the adoption and sale of children.

Zelizer's analysis is instructive in several ways. First, its focus is on ordinary people and the mundane life issues they confronted as they participated in historical transformation/lived their lives. Her description of the change in children's value from primarily economic to primarily sentimental also highlights the fundamentality of instrumentalism in the construction of children and childhood. Typically, psychologists use children to learn about adults or abstract laws of (human) nature or both. Practitioners are concerned to train children and their families in order to produce useful (productive, compliant, happy) adults. And parents, understandably, organize their activity to "bring up" their children, that is, to produce adults.

I intend this neither as evidence of a conspiracy nor as a glorification of children or childhood. Rather, I mean to show that the child constructed in and by Western culture has little integrity as a form of life. Childhood, seen as a phase or stage of life, is a means to an end called *adulthood*. Development is alienated—understood as a process (separate from its product) that must lead somewhere (better, higher). If it does not, it is not development proper. Development is understood as an abstraction related to another abstraction— "continuity" with our animal ancestors and/or our future selves and civilization. In my view, this is at odds with the human–social, relational activity of developing, which is neither hierarchical nor goal-oriented/directed but rather is continuously and nonpragmatically emergent.

The Child—Measurable and Adaptive

From the moment of its birth in the late 19th century, psychology found itself contending with strong pressure to abandon scientific discovery about the human condition (especially the mind) in favor of generating techniques and data that could be used by industry, education, and government leaders to further their pragmatic goals. Psychology's history is full of conflict, compromise, opportunism, deception, and deal-making as it became consumer-driven (the consumers being not the subjects of its research but those with the power to use its results to their advantage). The story of psychology is, among other things, a fascinating read (see, e.g., Baritz, 1960; Cushman, 1995; Danziger, 1994; Napoli, 1981; Newman & Holzman, 1996; Torrey, 1992). Instrumentalism won out rather early in the child study game, where the needs of educational administrators for methods of measurement and efficiency proved especially attractive for psychologists—and transformational for psychology. According to Danziger (1994):

> The attempt to apply psychology to the requirements of educational administration would have consequences for psychology that were far more profound than any contribution psychology was likely to make to education. In the first place, it meant a decisive break with the kind of educational psychology that had been envisaged by the pioneering giants of American psychology, by James, Baldwin, Hall, and Dewey. Their broader vision was now replaced by a much narrower and purely instrumental conception of what psychology could accomplish. The institutional constraints that the new educational psychologists took for granted required them to emphasize the passivity of the child and to restrict themselves to measured performance rather than wasting precious resources on an exploration of mental processes that had no obvious utility in terms of the goal of choosing the conditions that were most efficient in producing predetermined results. (pp. 104–105)

The dominance of quantification (and its underlying reductionism) helped set the stage for the enormous popularity of behaviorism in the United States in the middle of this century. Behaviorism, in turn, placed development on the back burner. Its tenets, laid out by John Watson as early as 1913, carved out behavior—not consciousness—as the subject matter of psychology and the prediction and control of behavior as its goal. Over the years, behaviorism's investigative practices became more sophisticated, but its underlying principle remained unchanged: All behavior could be accounted for in terms of conditioning, the association of stimulus and response.

Although behaviorism came to dominate experimental psychology as early as the 1930s, its practical application (e.g., in the treatment of mental illness and in education) did not become widespread until the 1950s and the popularity of B. F. Skinner. His highly speculative and grandiose claim that the most complex of human behavior can be explained, predicted, and controlled if the contingencies of reinforcement are known implies that development—qualitative change—does not occur or, at a minimum, is not a valid or necessary scientific construct. Everything is behavior, and behavior is everything. The countless (or infinite) number of things human beings do could be accounted for in terms derived from or reducible to simple laws of (animal) learning.

Interestingly, behaviorism was soundly refuted as a systematic scientific theory at the same time as its practical application began to increase. In

1959 the noted linguist Noam Chomsky wrote a definitive critique of Skinner's *Verbal Behavior* (1957) showing that contingencies of reinforcement could not possibly account for human language. Chomsky's essay was highly influential within the psychological research and psychological philosophy circles. Evidently, however, behaviorism's utility to institutional management, coupled with Skinner's persuasive arguments that behaviorist techniques were the key to social reform, proved too powerful to take scientific critique seriously—until Jean Piaget seemingly changed everything.

The Child—Active and Constructive

Jean Piaget, the Swiss biologist–philosopher–psychologist, is so integral to developmental psychology and teacher education that it is worth reminding ourselves of two features of his work: it did not begin to impact significantly on American intellectual life and pedagogical practice until the early 1960s; and it gave little attention to learning and instruction.

With the recognition of Piaget's prolific research over a 50-year period from the 1920s to the 1970s, developmental psychology came into its own. Knowledge claims about human development and about how we know what we know grew in sophistication and quantity. Developmental psychology had something new and creative to say, and thus it gained status among the diverse fields of psychology. Piaget was proudly philosophical, and this lent an element of intellectualism to what had been considered a "soft" and not very glamorous area of research (one, not incidentally, dominated by women up until this time).

The conception of the passive child was buried. Piaget's child is active. She or he does not adapt through responding to stimuli but assimilates and accommodates, constantly and actively adjusting the relationship between her or himself and the things, people, and events in the environment. In fact, the behaviorist conception of adaptation to environment becomes a nonissue, a given, or simply banal, as mental capacities, knowledge, and knowing gained center stage. Piaget's child does not receive knowledge of the world but invents or constructs it. Moreover, such an active being is not ignorant—gone is the notion that the child knows less than the adult. Piaget's child knows *differently* from the adult. Thus, the notion of qualitative change, rather than mere quantitative change, was introduced into the conception of development.

Without denying the changes brought about by Piaget's insights into cognition, his meticulous and fascinating observations, and his new method of investigation (more clinical than empirical), I do not think it unreasonable to view Piaget's primary impact as solidifying an idealized, ahistorical conception of the child. The Piagetian paradigm has been said to have contributed mightily to the naturalizing and normalizing of childhood

(Burman, 1994) and to the myth/hoax of psychology (Newman & Holzman, 1996). For Piaget did not relinquish any of the fundamental philosophical presuppositions already embedded within psychology (mind–body, in-ner–outer, knower–known duality; causality; and rationalism, to name a few). The Piagetian paradigm simply added to psychology's social construc-tion of the child, cementing (and liberalizing) the romanticized 19th century notion of the child as "other." Piaget's unique child, as we shall see, is uniquely abstract—a Cartesian–Kantian–Freudian human mentality.

By the Piagetian paradigm, I am referring not merely to Piaget's own large body of work, but to the continuation of his legacy (especially in the United States). Until recently, the stagist and structural elements of his theory dominated American research. The current shift in emphasis that focuses on his constructivism may be part of an effort to save Piagetian research from sinking into oblivion under the contemporary onslaught from two different (and opposed) forces: the post-Piagetian "infant as genius" move-ment, and the postmodern, social–constructionist and Vygotsky-influenced activity–theoretic movement(s).

Although it may be on the decline as a research paradigm, the Piagetian perspective permeates developmental psychology, educational theory and practice, and the wider culture (although it is not nearly as identifiable a presence there as Freudianism). The notion of invariant and linear stages of intellectual development, for example, is as much a part of the conception and understanding of growing up as is the belief in childhood psychic trauma. Piaget's ontology (the "stuff" of human psychological processes) is as much individuated as Freud's, and he has contributed just as significantly to the construction of the autonomous, individuated subject. Both presup-pose an inner–outer duality and the primacy of the biological as structurally and ontogenetically prior. Freud's individuated subject is in constant con-flict with the impinging "outside" (social world); this is the source of the individual personality. Piaget's individuated subject "assimilates" what is "outside"; this is the source of the individual knower. Piaget's active child is only instrumentally active. That is, the child's interaction with physical objects in the environment is a means to an end—it stimulates internal mental schema. The development of intelligence is, for Piaget, the devel-opment of knowing.

But what is meant by knowing? What are the criteria and standards by which the child's thinking is judged? Who is the quintessential knower? Piaget's model synthesized Western philosophical rationalism with psychol-ogy's mentalism and biology's reductionism. He not only turned Descartes' cogito ("I think, therefore I am") into a biologically determined psycho-logical reality, but also "succeeded in transforming each of the Kantian categories of knowledge from a first principle into a subject of scientific investigation" (Gruber & Voneche, 1977, p. xxix). For example, Piaget provided finely detailed observations of the emergence of the infant's concept of the object and development of object permanence, and he devoted entire books to investigating other Kantian categories, including space, time, and causality.

What Piaget means by thinking is logical thinking. When he described the child as thinking differently from the adult, he had a particular sort of adult, the modern scientist, in mind. The highest stage of intellectual development—*formal operations* (which is attained in adolescence, although not by everyone)—is reached when the child can perform a set of mental operations characteristic of the hypothetico-deductive model. The *formal operational child* who recognizes that a flattened ball of clay "is the same" or "has the same amount" as it did when it was round, Piaget asserted, has performed three mental operations on what he or she has perceived: identity, compensation, and inversion. The significance of this, intellectually speaking, is that only by carrying out these mental operations can the individual come to know (or construct knowledge of) the fact of the conservation of matter.

The resolution of contradiction plays an important role in Piaget's model of thinking and the child's growing ability to perform these mental operations. The *concrete operational child* first says that two balls of clay have the same amount, but upon seeing one ball flattened into a "snake" says it now has more (or less). Such a child is—so the Piagetian story goes—denying the contradiction between what he or she saw before and what he or she sees now and/or between what he or she sees (they do not look equal) and what he or she "knows" (no one added or took away any clay). The highest form of intellect, for Piaget, is "the growth of awareness of contradiction, the will to search for ways of thinking that can eliminate contradiction, in short the growth of logic" (Gruber & Voneche, 1977, p. xxi). The philosophical presupposition that identifies logic with thinking and relegates contradiction to a mental error has thus become woven into the fabric of psychology's conception of development.

The Piagetian child is also egocentric. Piaget's creative twist on Freud's concept of the ego was to transform this element of personality structure into a characteristic of early cognition. The child who cannot take the perspective of another is egocentric in both thinking and speaking. Preschool children playing side by side, for example, talk—but not to each other. Their speech is only superficially social; it lacks features that indicate awareness of the other person's point of view. Until the age of 7, speech is egocentric, that is, it is not communicative but "for oneself" (Piaget, 1955).

Piaget maintained that egocentric speech was evidence of egocentric thought: "This characteristic of a large portion of childish talk points to a certain egocentrism of thought itself.... And these thoughts are inexpressible precisely because they lack the means which are fostered only by the desire to communicate with others, and to enter into their point of view"

(Piaget, 1955, p. 206). Childhood egocentrism declines in one stage and reappears in another (from which it goes through another period of decline). The egocentric thought of the young child is thought that is unanalyzed and prelogical. It arises from things being schematized "in accordance with the child's own point of view, instead of being perceived in their intrinsic relations" (Piaget, 1955, p. 249). Thus, the child's view is narrow not only because it is personal relative to other people, but also because it does not take into account general laws and properties of objects.

Take Piaget's well-known "three mountain" task. A child of a certain age is placed before a model of three mountains that vary in height and other features. A doll is placed so that it has a different "view" of the mountains. The child is asked to describe first what she or he sees and then what the doll sees. The egocentric child cannot "take the doll's point of view" (cannot perform the necessary mental operations on the objects of perception—e.g., transforming the objects in space), but simply repeats the first description to describe what the doll sees.

Piaget's claims about egocentrism rest on and perpetuate the presuppositions of duality and causality—his analysis is based on the dichotomy of inner–outer/private–social worlds, and an assumed parallelism between causal mechanisms that operate in the physical and the mental realms. Piaget's inner–outer duality is essentially psychoanalytic; to account for the transitions from egocentric to social speech and from egocentric thinking to logical thinking, he had to introduce "needs." Accordingly, the child's world is really two worlds—that of inner needs and objective reality. The young, egocentric child is motivated to satisfy only inner needs; development in thought is the gradual adaptation to outer reality. Anticipating the discussion in chapter 3 of Vygotsky's nondualistic perspective on development, some of Vygotsky's (1987) critique follows:

> When Piaget borrowed Freud's concept that the pleasure principle precedes the reality principle, he adopts the whole metaphysic associated with the concept of the pleasure principle. Here the principle is transformed from an auxiliary or biologically subordinate characteristic into a kind of independent vital force, into the prime mover of the whole process of mental development. (p. 77)

Vygotsky (1987) went on to reject Piagetian/Freudian duality, pointing to the problems inherent in assuming a separation between satisfying needs and adapting to reality. In doing so, he exposed the passivity of Piaget's supposedly active child:

> Piaget has argued that things do not influence the mind of the child. But we have seen that where the child's egocentric speech is linked to his practical activity, where it is linked to his thinking, things really do operate on his mind and influence it. By the word "things" we mean reality. However, what we have in mind is *not reality as it is passively reflected in perception or abstractly cognized*. We mean reality as it is encountered in practice. (p. 79, italics added)

The Child—Social and Related

Vygotsky and those influenced by him are not the only psychologists to find Piaget's assumptions troublesome. Earlier, I referred to alternatives to Piaget's paradigm, including neo-Piagetian constructivism and social constructionism. During the 1970s, the growing fascination of developmentalists with "the social world" coincided with emerging doubts about Piaget's asocial child. New experimental and observational technology (such as video, film, and other equipment for measuring eye movements, rates of sucking, and other physical and physiological behavior) made it possible for infants and babies to be scrutinized in ways they never could before. The importance of social interaction (usually identified or idealized as the mother–child dyad) was recognized. The assumptions and goals of developmental psychology were modified to take into account the fact that the child lives in a "social world." Let us now examine some of the knowledge claims and investigative practices of this new approach to see if it in fact has succeeded in ridding psychology of its philosophical presuppositions, its bifurcation of life activity into the biological and the social, and its evolutionary bias.

In *Deconstructing Developmental Psychology*, Burman (1994) critically analyzed the developmental psychology of the past 25 years. She described how recent research tries to overcome the split between the biological and social but ultimately fails, in part because it cannot give up its evolutionary framework. In Burman's view, the contemporary developmental psychologist conceptualizes the infant as a biological organism "equipped with a reflexive repertoire of behaviours that function to elicit care, nurturance and attention. This is interpreted … as being of 'survival value' to the species as well as to the individual (since the individual is portrayed as the species' future)" (p. 35). The way in which subtle differences in infants' behavior elicit a fine-tuning of their caregivers' responses to their needs is cited as evidence of the children's readiness for adaptation to social interaction. One example is the way mothers quickly learn to respond differentially to their infants' crying patterns. The child is thus seen as "prewired" to make the gradual shift from a biological to a social being.

As Burman (1994) pointed out, what the researchers have accomplished is not the elimination of the biological–social/inner–outer duality, but its reinforcement. The suggestion that development takes place "from lesser to greater involvement with and awareness of the social world" conjures up "the image of a transition from isolation into sociality, with the epithet 'social' qualifying 'world' functioning retrospectively to designate the world the child had previously inhabited as pre- or non-social" (p. 36).

Piaget's infant recapitulated the universal, predetermined general laws that supposedly govern the intellectual development of the species. The "outer world" was required so that it could be manipulated by the infant, thereby making it possible for internal mental structures of thought to transform. In this way, the child's development is individually and autono-mously self-constructed. Social interaction with other human beings be-came an important factor in development only in middle childhood.

In contrast, the neo- and post-Piagetian infant is individualistically *predisposed* to sociality. It is not only the caregiver who is attuned to the infant's mental states and behavioral subtleties; the infant, too, is capable of detecting and interpreting the caregiver's behavior. The driving force of development is no longer Kantian categories or Freudian intrapsychic conflict. Now development is propelled by our inherent socialness, the necessity of living in a social world. This new conception of development required new psychological objects such as *mutual intentionality, intersubjec-tivity,* and *relatedness* which, in turn, became the subject of research and the source of new knowledge claims. For example, an innate predisposition for cooperative turn-taking is inferred from the way infants and mothers synchronize their body movements (Kaye, 1982; Trevarthan & Hubley, 1978). This primitive form of relatedness is said to lay the groundwork for later discourse.

No matter how "predisposed" we are to sociality, the question still remains—within this dualistic perspective—as to how we actually become social. For some psychologists, it is discourse—seen as the arena for (or instrument of) the coming together of the private and the social—that provides a clue. Employing a narrative or dialogic perspective (sometimes attributed to Bakhtin, 1981), they attempt to show, empirically, how adult and child must create intersubjectivity. Infants and babies who were once said to be responding verbally to stimuli, expressing meanings, or processing information are now said to be learning to "transcend" their "private world" as they verbally interact or dialogue with the significant adults in their environment.

For example, in the 1980s the American Vygotskian James Wertsch conducted a series of studies employing what he called a microgenetic analysis of mother–child dyads completing a puzzle-copying task—for him, a cognitive task. In analyzing how they put the puzzle together, Wertsch argued that carrying out this kind of productive joint cognitive activity requires entering into a certain level of intersubjectivity (Wertsch, 1985a, p. 175).

We can see how the concepts of intersubjectivity and joint activity maintain psychology's bifurcation of inner–outer and private–social from the way Wertsch interpreted mother–child discourse. In one dyad that failed to put the puzzle together, the child continued to refer to the circular objects as circles and crackers in spite of the fact that his mother called them wheels. Wertsch (1985a) gave the following interpretation:

> A cursory examination of this excerpt reveals that the child was not very successful at "transcending his private world." He apparently never understood that the pieces

represented wheels on a truck. It seems that throughout the interaction he viewed the pieces as circles or crackers rather than as wheels. Because of the child's constant inability to negotiate or "buy into" a situation definition that would be more appropriate for carrying out this culturally defined task, the adult was forced to adjust her communicative moves such that they could be interpreted within his alternative framework. (pp. 172–173)

Wertsch's main point was to show that mothers use semiotic mechanisms (to adjust their language as, for example, "the truck wheels," "yes, they're like circles," "one like that one") in creating joint cognitive activity with their children. However, it does not follow from the fact that "wheels" might be more culturally *appropriate* than "circles" or "crackers" in this experimenter-defined task that "wheels" is any less a cultural phenomenon. Yet, the presumptions of a dualistically divided world, private mental states, and Freudian psychodynamics are apparent in Wertsch's assertion that the child could not transcend his "private world" and use of terms like "buy into," "forced," "negotiate," and "alternative framework." The attempt to establish intersubjectivity as a requirement for joint activity involves Wertsch in making highly questionable claims such as that "circle" and "crackers" lie in the secret depths of the child's alienated and bifurcated inner life, and that the child has an "alternative framework." What evidence is there that the child has *any* framework at all? Why do we need to posit the existence of a framework from which to interpret "communicative moves"? Do we, in fact, ordinarily "interpret communicative moves" when we engage in discourse?

An alternative way of seeing joint activity that does not rest on the presumption of a knowing mind is that the mothers are responding to the relational activity of speaking together, to the creative meaning making of their discourse/dialogue/narrative. From this activity–theoretic vantage point, intersubjectivity is not a requirement for joint activity. It *is* joint activity.

In an attempt to avoid the scientific and philosophical pitfalls inherent in attributing motives and intentionality to infants and very young children, some developmental psychologists adopt the position that Burman (1994) called "as if." That is, they argue that adults treat babies "as if they were fully initiated social partners, as if they were able to participate in a social system" (p. 39). They account for development with the claim that "by treating the infant as socially competent … she becomes so" (p. 39).

Burman summarized what, in her opinion, is one of the more promising versions of this view, Kaye's (1982) *The Mental and Social Life of Babies*. Her summary and critique help us to see just how deep-rooted are the evolutionary, dualistic, and causal presuppositions of developmental theory. According to Burman, Kaye gets off to a good start by asserting that the infant is "born social in the sense that his [sic] development will depend from the beginning upon patterns of interaction with elders" (Kaye, 1982, p. 29, cited in Burman, 1994,

p. 40). When the infant comes to have expectations about these patterns of interaction (e.g., expectations of what the mother will do), then it can be said that mother and infant are a social system. These expectations are not genetically programmed, but arise out of experience. The social system is thus a joint construction of mother and child.

Burman presented Kaye's discussion of one of the earliest instances of such a social system—the pattern of interaction in breast feeding. Apparently, the infant sucks in bursts and pauses, and the mother has a "tendency to jiggle the nipple of her breast (or the teat of the bottle) during the pauses." To Kaye, the combination of these patterns "constitutes the earliest form of mutual adaptation and turn-taking" (Burman, 1994, p. 41). What is happening is that the mother is treating her infant as a turn-taker—creating turns to take and setting up patterns—and the infant "will start to take her own turn and assume her place in the social world" (Burman, 1994, p. 41).

Burman's issues with Kaye (aside from gender and cultural biases in his descriptions) are many. For one thing, he perpetuated the very biological–social opposition he attempted to transcend. Mothers' jiggling and infants' sucking and pausing are biological givens that come to function as social. Furthermore, the interactional patterns turn out to be products of evolution "every bit as much as those features we think of as innate to the individual organism" (Kaye, 1982, p. 24, cited in Burman, 1994, p. 42). Human sociality is thereby made understandable in terms of evolution. Burman further pointed out that although Kaye did not posit any explicit causality between early and later developments, he nevertheless identified a basic unit (turn-taking) that "becomes the building block for everything else" (p. 42). It is worth adding that in doing so, Kaye reproduced the reductionistic form of theory-building that seeks one explanatory principle for all of development; he insisted that there be a pattern to patterns.

In these ways, Burman helps us to see that psychology's construction of the socially situated and socially competent infant has not gotten us very far from Darwin's son: development is *still* seen as driven by evolution, by an anachronistic functionalist biology (Gould, 1996; Morss, 1995). Certainly this is important to see if we are to understand the myth of development that psychology has constructed and its influence within education. There are, in addition, other problems with the socially competent and socially situated infant to consider. Burman and other critics of psychology's conception of development point out its ideological and political biases, for example, its attempt to preserve the status quo, its Eurocentrism, its glorification of the middle class "ideal," its presumption of female inferiority, and its glorification of heterosexuality (in addition to Burman, 1994, see Bulhan, 1985; Burman, 1990; Cushman, 1991; Gilligan, 1982; Singer, 1993; Walkerdine, 1984, 1988). Such work has played a role in motivating investigations of developmental psychology's philosophical and methodological biases. The philosophical presuppositions that developmental psychology wittingly or unwittingly accepts—mentalism, rationalism, causality, duality, linearity, beginning and endpoints, particularity, interpretation, and explanation—as the rationale for its investigative practices and knowledge claims are themselves gender-, class-, and culturally biased.

PSYCHOLOGICAL MEASUREMENT
CONSTRUCTS THE LEARNER

The idealized images of the child, childhood, and development that psychology constructed over the course of the 20th century were consistent with the emerging culture, social organization, and politics. Indeed, psychology was and is a most powerful carrier of ideology—it determines how we think about what it means to be human, what it means to grow, think, speak, and feel, and even what it means to mean. Individualism, identity, mentalism, and causation are conceptions that, for better or worse, give shape to everyday human experience and, although these conceptions do not belong solely to psychology, they undoubtedly owe much of their currency to the discipline. What role do these conceptions play in our understanding and experience of learning? How has psychology constructed (our image of) "the learner"? From the beginnings of educational and school psychology in the first decades of the 20th century, through the dominance of the Piagetian paradigm and the subsequent "cognitive revolution" of the 1960s, 1970s, and 1980s, the epistemological paradigm (knowing) that is embedded in psychology has powerfully determined the structure, organization, and experience of schooling. In this way, the philosophical structure of schooling is inseparable from psychology's construction of learning, just as it is inseparable from psychology's construction of development.

The earliest interventions of psychologists into education had little to do with educational goals. Rather, they originated from the child study and mental hygiene movements. As early as the 1890s, psychologists gained the cooperation of teachers in order to conduct large-scale, census-type studies of psychological traits of children at different ages in order to discover what were believed to be evolutionary laws of nature. The turn-of-the-century mental hygiene movement had begun with efforts to change the barbaric treatment of people deemed mentally ill by reforming "lunatic asylums." The mental hygienists believed that social and interpersonal problems were a consequence of childhood maladjustment and could be ameliorated through the intervention of appropriate agencies of social control. Understandably, they became interested in child care and educational institutions. The mental hygiene movement was generously supported by grants, many for school interventions, from private foundations throughout the 1920s (Danziger, 1994; Rivlin & Wolfe, 1985).

At the same time, the techniques devised during World War I to test the intelligence of military recruits enabled psychologists to make a new kind of knowledge claim. The legitimacy psychology gained from the Army mental testing project was profound, especially in light of the fact that it was both a scientific and practical failure. (Among the many sources of the history and analysis of mental testing in the United States, Danziger, 1994; Kamin, 1974; Lawler, 1978; and Samelson, 1979, make especially fascinating reading). By the end of the war, all 48 states had passed compulsory education legislation, and educational administrators were faced with the daunting task of running very large educational institutions. In attempting to create an industrial-style educational system, their concern was with efficiency; accordingly, they turned to the "experts," the psychologists, for help in doing their jobs. They wanted to know how to sort pupils, who was smart and who was not, who would succeed, how to speed up learning, manage the flow of pupils and subject matter, and answers to other pragmatic and often self-serving questions.

In his study of the historical origins of psychological research, Danziger (1994) suggested that these institutional needs of educational administrators played a significant role in the invention of what today is psychology's mainstay, the *treatment group*. Schools provided ready-made groups of children who could be placed under differing conditions of instruction and whose performance could be measured both before and after the intervention. Rather quickly, such group treatment was brought into the laboratory. In this way, the two earliest methods of psychological investigation, laboratory experimentation and the aggregating of date (which originated in intelligence testing) were merged. To Danziger, this pragmatically driven investigative practice contributed mightily to psychology's invention of new knowledge claims—about something called "learning capacity":

> In the safety of university laboratories a kind of experimentation that had originated in relatively mundane practical concerns developed into a vehicle for maintaining fantasies of an omnipotent science of human control. In their original school settings experiments based on treatment groups could be of some practical value because the institutional context provided a known and consistent framework for applying the results. But the more ambitious American psychologists were not content with the humble role of psychological technician. To them the performance of children on school tasks under different conditions was simply one instance of the operation of generalized "laws of learning" that manifested themselves in the entire game of human behavior. This faith enabled them to continue to use a style of experimentation that had already proved its practical usefulness and to reinterpret the results of such experimentation so they now provided evidence bearing on the fundamental laws of behavior. They imagined that what they observed in these experiments were not specific effects depending on a host of special conditions but the operation of a few highly abstract principles of organismic learning or forgetting. (pp. 115–116)

Once psychology got hold of this abstraction called learning, it was reluctant to abandon it. After all, until the normalizing (and humanizing) of abnormality during the first half of the 20th century—the invention of neurosis, the popularization of Freudianism, the public recognition of (and government legislation designed to promote) something called mental health—gave psychology something else about which to claim exclusive expertise, general laws of learning were its best-selling product (Newman & Holzman, 1996). The conception of learning as the *quantifiable and measurable behavior of individuals* (although individuals as individuals are rarely actually studied) that obeys natural and universal laws contains the same philosophical and political biases as psychology's conception of development. It also illustrates the way psychology gained its legitimacy from its data-generating capabilities and technical–statistical creations, rather than from serious scientific theorizing (Danziger, 1994). For in spite of its claims, it is questionable whether mainstream, scientific psychology has ever produced a bona fide theory of human learning.

Psychology's conception of learning is nothing if not consistently dualistic. The inner–outer, person–environment, individual–social, consciousness–behavior dualities are ever-present. Behaviorism (which eschewed anything mentalistic) and cognitive science and information processing theories (which postulate internal mental processes as explanatory) are two sides of the same dualistic coin. Social learning theory, as its name implies, retained the bifurcation between the individual and the social. (Why else identify *social* learning?) Piagetian theory and even neo-Piagetian constructivism, in taking learning to involve the construction of knowledge by the child, also presuppose the above dualities.

Through most of the first half of this century when behaviorism dominated scientific psychology, learning was closely identified with adaptation and training. Human learning was not thought to differ in kind from animal learning. Psychologists holding to seemingly contradictory foundational beliefs—inherent ability (intelligence) on the one hand and universal mechanisms of adaptation (behavioral laws) on the other hand—produced tens of thousands of research studies comparing the performance of rats, pigeons, and human beings on thousands of laboratory learning tasks. The result was the production of hundreds of knowledge claims about newly "discovered" psychological objects, such as learning curves, transfer effects, contingencies of reinforcement, latent learning and the like. Many of these psychological findings were applied educationally in the structuring of classrooms and classroom practices, the design of textbooks, curricula, and other instructional materials, and the construction of tests and other measures of evaluation.

Despite Piaget's relative lack of interest in learning and instruction—he saw learning as outside intervention that is subordinate to (dependent on) a person's level of development—his work had a significant impact on how psychologists and educators think about learning. It was Piaget's delineation of the structural changes in the child's mind as she or he developed intellectually that transformed the conception of learning (Miller, 1993). As his writings became popular in the 1960s, the importance of knowledge was reintroduced into the family of concepts associated with learning. For the behaviorists, knowledge was not a relevant concept. Knowing and related concepts, such as understanding, thinking, and meaning were, from a behaviorist perspective, scientifically meaningless and unnecessary in order to account for human behavior and action. Learning was associated with things animals and people *did*, that is, with changes in behaviors (both the acquisition of new ones and the modification of old ones). Piaget's substantial body of research on children's thinking contributed to psychologists (and later educators) coming to associate learning with the acquisition of new knowledge—with knowledge redefined as the ability to reason about things, that is, as conceptual rather than factual. Prior to Piaget, the psychological task was to account for how a child could be trained to count to 10. After Piaget, the psychological task was to account for how the child acquired knowledge of numbers (*the concept of number*), and to recognize that this process was gradual and occurred in fixed stages. (Again, for Piaget this was not a question of learning but one of development.)

The educational issues that emerged from this changed perspective were two-fold: whether it was possible and, if so, how to facilitate the acquisition of new knowledge; and how to develop educational practices consistent with Piaget's claims about children's thinking and stages of development. For example, Kohlberg and Mayer (1972) argued that a Piagetian cognitive–developmental perspective (integrated with some of Dewey's views) should be the basis for setting educational objectives. What has resulted from adopting a Piagetian model in education has been, more often than not, a consistent underestimation of what children can do. According to Brown (1994), it "encourages sensitivity to what children of a certain age *cannot* do because they have not yet reached a certain stage of cognitive operations" (p. 10).

What emerged (gradually and more in principle than in practice, given how resistant to change the institution of education is) was a shift from content-oriented to process-oriented pedagogy. The task of teachers was no longer to impart information and to train children in reading, writing, and math skills but to help them—as their minds developed more logically sophisticated powers of reasoning and conceptualizing—learn "spontaneously" and discover "on their own" how the world works. The object of educational practice became "the developing child." Piaget opened the door for cognitive psychology and the full-blown revival of mentalism.

As interest and financial support for cognitive and information-processing research grew in the 1970s and 1980s, what came to dominate educational theorizing was the notion that children's success or failure as learners has to do with their mental processes—their memory, perceptual, conceptual, and problem-solving abilities. Psychological researchers devised sophisticated technology to generate data on the way the human mind works: how information is stored and retrieved; how adults and children solve problems; how language is processed and so on. Laboratory findings were said to reveal that human cognition is exquisitely systematic. The mind was analogized to a highly complex and finely tuned machine, an apparatus that applies specific mental operations in specific ways to specific types of information that "come in." Models of hypothetical mental operations and rules of mental representation were posited. Certain of these mental operations were seen as foundational to learning to read, write, and do arithmetic. Thus, school tasks came to be understood as *requiring a certain level of cognitive development*. Learning depended on thinking and reasoning.

The "discovery" of foundational mental abilities of both Piagetian and cognitive research led to a reconceptualization of how knowledge is acquired—it is not transmitted, but constructed. As Brown (1994) put it in her presidential address to the American Educational Research Association: "Learners came to be viewed as active constructors, rather than passive recipients of knowledge. Learners were imbued with powers of introspection, once verboten. One of the most interesting things about human learning is that we have knowledge and feelings about it, sometimes even control over it, *metacognition* if you will" (p. 6).

It is this model of the learner as active constructor of knowledge that has come to dominate educational research. *Constructivism* (the learning model) and *constructivist pedagogy* (curricula, instructional, and evaluation practices) are the subject of many research studies and demonstration projects. They are also the subject of much contemporary debate: Does constructivism reinforce an individualistic understanding of the learning process? Does it ignore the societal, cultural, and political nature of schooling and learning? Does it blunt efforts to examine the nature and quality of the knowledge that is being constructed? (See the article by Hiebert et al., and responses to it in *Educational Researcher*, 1996, pp. 4–23).

Developmentally appropriate education also follows from the conception of the learner as an active constructor of knowledge. According to Elkind (1991), the goal of developmentally appropriate education is "to produce creative, critical thinkers. This is not achieved by teaching children and adolescents thinking skills, but rather by creating developmentally appropriate learning environments that will encourage and challenge the child's emerging mental abilities" (p. 8). The influence of this approach, however, has been largely confined to early childhood education. The idea is to match instructional style and curriculum to the developmental level of the child, taking into account cognitive, social, emotional, and physical development. In the process of actively constructing knowledge, children—it is presumed—are using "higher order thinking skills."

Summarizing some of the leading proponents of developmentally appro-priate education, Rust (1993) noted the following anticipated results: children will develop understanding, problem-solving skills, independent thinking, and "awareness of their own cultural backgrounds as well as the diversity of perspectives that inform most problems"; schools will serve as "adaptive learning environments that are sensitive to the individual needs of children and to their family and cultural backgrounds ... rather than schools molding children to fit their structures" (pp. 6–7). This kind of "child-centered" approach—where instruction is individualized, contextu-alized, interactionist, and constructivist—is offered as a powerful and effec-tive alternative to homogenous and rigid, rote learning.

But where does this alternative lead? Is the actively constructivist learner any less an individuated subject than the passive learner? Isn't basing the curriculum and mode of instruction on measures of presumed developmen-tal level still a way that schools are "molding children to fit their struc-tures"—in other words, isn't it just the structures that have been changed? Aren't "the individual needs of children" still understood as knowledge-based, cognitive, and rational—and, if so, doesn't that violate the stated principle of openness to a variety of perspectives that inform problems? Finally, doesn't developmentally appropriate education embody internal contradictions? If human beings construct knowledge, then isn't it the *active construction*—not the environment—that is "developmentally appropri-ate?" If "the environment" out of which human beings, presumably, con-struct knowledge is determined by others, wherein lies the "active construction?" These questions are meant to point to ways that the reform of identifying learning with becoming a thinker (even if a "creative, critical thinker") reinforces, rather than challenges, the Eurocentric conception of what it means—and how human beings come—to know.

For all the research reports and books delineating this new way of seeing children, knowledge, learning, and what should go on in schools, the impact of these reforms on mass education has been relatively minor. The image of the learner has certainly changed—not only educators, but ordinary people tend to think of a learner as an information processor, a constructor of knowledge, a problem solver, a critical thinker. Indeed, that human beings are like computers has become as much a part of Western culture as the belief in the ego. (The irony of the computer analogy is that the original question of whether machines could be designed to think like people has been turned around on us.) But have school practices (or even parent expectations, for that matter) transformed?

To the extent that school organization and classroom practices have come to reflect the discovery of "the developing child," the changes are largely confined to early childhood and kindergarten programs. Most mid-dle, intermediate, and high schools still track students into classrooms based on prior achievement, teach to informational tests, and maintain an interactional mode consisting of whole group instruction coupled with individual book work (the thousands of government and foundation-funded intervention and demonstration projects conducted by educational researchers affiliated with universities and "think tanks" notwithstanding). Despite the change in perspective from "behavior" to "mind," from product to process, and from passive to active, what Freire called "the banking system" of education (1972) still flourishes in American schools.

The conceptions of the learner and learning constructed by psychology, along with the instructional practices that follow from them, have not gone unchallenged. Critics of the banking system of education and the cognitive psychology-influenced reforms have been making their views known for at least 30 years—by now, thousands of books and articles have been published. Writers within the traditions of radical pedagogy and critical pedagogy center their arguments on the political purposes and ideological biases of education in general and on the race, class, and gender biases inherent in the conception of the ahistorical, idealized, individuated learner in particular. More identified with sociology—the sociology of education and the sociology of knowledge—than psychology, radical and critical educators often draw upon the writings of Marxist, feminist, or Third World revolutionary thinkers, and present their own work as part of the ongoing political struggle against the race, class, and gender oppression of Euro-American domination.[2]

Mind "in" Society

The somewhat newer trends of *sociocultural* or *cultural–historical psychology* and *activity theory* are primarily challenges to the dominant methodology (and, in general, are consistent with the spirit of ideological critiques). Their focus is on how schools, educational practices, and psychological research have misidentified the very nature of human learning by ignoring its cultural and social–historical nature. The 1970s work of the Rockefeller University Laboratory of Comparative Human Cognition, mentioned in chapter 1, was a place of origin for this new approach to understanding learning. Recall the lab's guiding question: "How come kids who are 'street smart' are 'school dumb'?" We were concerned to discover some things about so-called "cognitive events"—what is it about how they are organized outside of school that produces so many successful displays of knowledge and skill, and how are they organized in school settings to produce so many displays of failure.

We identified as a significant factor the manner in which the presupposition of "private mental acts" overdetermines both social interaction and how analysts look at social interaction within school settings (Cole, Hood,

---

[2]Among early seminal works and well-known recent writings are: Apple (1979), Bowles and Gintis (1976), Fine (1991, 1994), Giroux (1983, 1993), Greer (1972), hooks (1994), and McLaren (1989, 1995).

& McDermott, 1978; Hood, McDermott, & Cole, 1980; McDermott & Hood, 1982). In the ongoing development of research projects, the lab made use of the methods of various fields and insights of diverse voices, including early proponents of a human science approach (pre-20th-century critics of positivism), cultural anthropologists and ethnographers, and pioneers in cybernetics. But it was, and remains, the works of Vygotsky and other Soviet/Russian philosophers, psychologists, and linguists (e.g., Bakhtin, Leontiev, Luria, and Davydov) that have especially influenced those with a social–cultural–historical perspective.

To proponents of cultural historical activity theory (CHAT; a term that gained popularity in 1996), psychological processes such as thinking, speaking, literacy, and problem solving are best understood as *cultural practices* that reflect the *historical development* of the human species. Moreover, they are always *socially situated and socially distributed* and shaped by, or come into existence through, *mediational means* (e.g., the use of such tools as language, computers, number systems, or a string tied around one's finger). Human learning is taken to be the process of the *appropriation of cultural tools* that occurs through *joint activity in communities of practice*.

The foundation for this characterization (although not the language of it) owes much to Vygotsky's sociocultural theory. To put it more accurately, it owes much to a specific reading of Vygotsky that prevails in the United States and, increasingly, internationally—a reading initially and most consistently put forth by Cole and his colleagues (Cole, 1985, 1995; Cole & Engestrom, 1993; Newman, Griffin, & Cole, 1989) and by James Wertsch (1985a, 1991)—recall Wertsch's analysis of the joint activity of the puzzle task. This reading takes Vygotsky to be offering a powerful alternative to both behaviorism and Piagetian constructivism as explanations of learning and increasing cognitive ability. In place of behavioristic determinism and an abhorrence of consciousness, Vygotsky insisted that learning and cognition have everything to do with consciousness—consciousness being a sociocultural product/activity of human history. In place of Piagetian inside-the-head mental schemas possessed by self-contained individuals, Vygotsky did not merely add the social and cultural "aspects" of learning and cognitive activity, but insisted that they are social and cultural. The unit that engages in learning and cognition is not "the individual" but the unity person-and-environment ("mind in society"), where environment and society are not abstractions but real people. In order to find out what a child knows, it is necessary to see what she or he does in collaboration with others rather than alone. This claim of Vygotsky's might itself be the most radical challenge to psychological theorizing about "the learner" and schooling practices ever made.

Psychological functions, for Vygotsky, initially appear as relations between people and become "internalized." They are jointly created. For example, adults and children are constantly engaging in activities together. The adults are more advanced and skilled (e.g., at speaking and problem solving) than children. Through their interaction, they engage in the activity (or complete the task) in such a way that children creatively imitate the more advanced adults. This joint creation of the imitative activity—a critical part of what Vygotsky called the zone of proximal development (ZPD)—*is* learning and development.

Critical to Vygotsky's notions of learning and cognitive activity is the fact of tool use. Not only do human beings make and use tools such as hammers and knives, we also make and use psychological tools (such as language). Psychological tools were important to Vygotsky because it is through creating and using them that we change ourselves and our culture. Speaking and language were, to Vygotsky, the psychological tools most critical to human development because of their importance in human history and culture and because of their ongoing role in creating thinking (conceptualization, generalization) and other psychological processes. It is in this sense that Vygotsky speaks of learning and cognitive growth as mediated.

The term *activity theory* is often associated with Vygotsky, although this psychological approach did not develop until after his death. One source of the Soviet concept of activity is the Marxist understanding of the transformative nature of labor activity. According to Marx, it is through labor that human beings overcome the split between the objective world (nature) and the subjective world. Labor activity is a source of human social development and of community (see Kozulin, 1990). Perhaps more important was Marx's methodological challenge to the idealism and mentalism inherent in the objective–subjective split that dominated philosophical thought as, for example, when he described "human activity itself as *objective* activity ... as 'revolutionary,' or 'practical–critical' activity" (Marx, 1973, p. 121). Contemporary debates among psychologists about activity theory bear little connection with Marx's argument. They are concerned with abstractions that have to do with levels of analysis (activity, action, and operation) posited by the leading developer of activity theory, Leontiev (who was a student of Vygotsky's).

This, briefly, is a summary of what most sociocultural, cultural–historical, and activity–theoretic psychologists take to be significant in Vygotsky's writings and what they utilize in the many theoretical discussions, analyses of classroom practices, curricular recommendations, and intervention projects that have appeared since the late 1980s.[3] In the following two chapters, we examine much of what they have ignored.

---

[3]See Cole (1985, 1990); Cole and Engestrom (1993); Hedegaard, Hakkarainen, and Engestrom (1984); Kozulin (1990); Levitin (1982); Newman, Griffin and Cole (1989); Newman and Holzman (1993); Steward (1995); Ratner (1991); Rogoff (1990); Tharp and Gallimore (1988); van der Veer and Valsiner (1991); and Wertsch (1985b, 1991); as well as articles in the edited volumes by Chaiklin and Lave (1993); Daniels (1993, 1996); Dixon-Krauss (1996); John-Steiner, Panofsky, and Smith (1994); Moll (1990); Rogoff and Lave (1984); and Wertsch (1985a).

Part II

A New Cultural, Performatory Psychology

◆ ◆ ◆

In Part I, I attempted to bring into view the underlying philosophical structure of education, the manner in which the conceptions of learning and development constructed by psychology determine the way schooling in America is done and, additionally, how they can limit the impact of contemporary challenges to traditional educational models. The centuries-old cognitive bias of Western thought is alive and well. We just cannot seem to give up *knowing* and *knowers*. We appear to be incapable of escaping Western culture's glorification of human cognitive processes (even, or especially, those "jointly constructed")—the primacy of thought over action, the value of critical consciousness and critical faculties, knowing, knowing *about*, and *aboutness* in general. This obsessive concern with seeking and producing knowledge, in my opinion, is stifling of ongoing developmental activity especially—but not exclusively—in schools.

But can we possibly understand anything if we do not depend on knowing? How and what would we learn? Is there such a thing as nonepistemological (nonknowing) understanding? I think so. It is a kind of understanding (and learning) that is indistinguishable from participating in the life process. Very young children "do understanding" in this way; they actually become knowers fairly late in the process of adaptation. For functioning as a knower requires a certain distance between oneself as the knower and what is to be known, and infants and babies simply lack this distance; their understanding (and learning) is inseparable from their on-going activity. The distance between knower and known (which we can call intrapsychic epistemological alienation) emerges gradually with societal–cultural adaptation (Bakhurst, 1991). As we shall see in chapter 3, growing without knowing is, in fact, critical for all kinds of developments in early childhood, especially those that are essential for societal adaptation—including, ironically, the adaptation to knowing. Reinitiating the human activity of developing—at any age—requires, in my opinion, rejecting knowing as the sole or dominant form of understanding.

Closely linked to the Western commitment to knowing is an equally strong commitment to the concept of the individual (and her or his "knowing mind"). The *individual*, in turn, is related to the notion of *the particular*, a conception psychology adopted from philosophy that has become embedded in the philosophical structure of education.

Psychology is fond of (some would say obsessed with) dividing the totality of continuous human experience into pieces (particulars). Human life, supposedly, consists of distinct time periods (infancy, early childhood, the middle years and so on). Human functioning is said to comprise several distinct processes (such as perception, memory, and cognition). Each of these processes is said to have its own developmental course (such as physiological development, perceptual development, emotional development, and cognitive development). This practice (called reductionism by its critics) is justified by appealing to *the scientific method* as if it were a sacred text on the order of the Ten Commandments or the Magna Carta—rather than an idealized rendition of conventions more or less loosely followed in the physical sciences until even there they were abandoned (e.g., in physics) when inquiries into the history, sociology, and philosophy of science revealed that the way scientists work is more unsystematic than systematic.[1] Isolating variables, reducing things to their supposedly essential elements, measuring them, and then, perhaps, putting it all together again—this is the way, we have been told since elementary school, to make discoveries about human beings.

Alternatively, there is the pragmatic rationalization, the apologetic "You can't study everything!" This claim (like its counterpart, "You can't change the world!") is not only politically conservative; it is methodologically prescientific. It is grounded in notions that are as old as Western philosophy itself. Conceptions that were devised by the ancient Greeks to account for the human capacities of self-consciousness and abstracting have transformed dramatically over two centuries. Yet they are still with us. *How* we think about truth, reality, certainty, and cause has changed. *That* we still think in these terms is undeniable.

The ancient Greek notion of *the particular*—the presupposition that what exists, and what is knowable, are particular things—is one of the things that underlies our commitment to knowing. When Aristotle, through his logic of particularity and identity, cemented the world as divided in two—ontology (what exists or is to be known) and epistemology (the who and how of

---

[1]See, for example, Burt (1954), *The Metaphysical Foundations of Modern Science*, and Kuhn (1970), *The Structure of Scientific Revolutions.*

knowing)—he also defined epistemology in relation to particularity. Uniting what had been, to Plato, the mystical world of forms and the world of substance, Aristotle said that particulars (earthly objects) contain *both* form and substance. We human beings understand, or know, earthly objects because the form that shapes their substance (such as the wood of a chair) also shapes the substance of our minds (the consciousness of chair). In other words, both the chair and our consciousness of it are shaped by the same reality. Understanding or knowing thus derives from harmony of the individual and the thing.

In the 13th century, Aristotle's ideas were used to recreate Christianity (mainly by Thomas Aquinas), but their influence spread much wider than religious thought. During the complex transition from the premodern to the modern era when scientific rationality gradually replaced religious teleology, some elements of Aristotle's worldview were abandoned. But the core conception and logic of static particulars were not. Modern science brought a new view of the world—as being naturally in motion rather than naturally at rest, a new view of "Man"—as uniquely *other than* Nature, and a new view of their relationship—the universe was governed by rules which Man alone can make and know and by which he can, thereby, establish control over it. Human beings thus came to be characterized as knowers (viewers, perceivers, technological interveners) of the world; in fact, our very existence and identity became contingent on our knowing, or epistemic, capabilities (see Newman & Holzman, 1996).

Aristotle's way of formulating these epistemic capabilities was in terms of particulars. Knowing consists of deducing or logically inferring one thing (a particular about a particular) from another (another particular). This came to define "proper thinking." In this way reasoning about things remained essentially static, classificatory, and deductive—even if the things themselves were constantly in motion.

This epistemological paradigm has been the basis for remarkable advances in the biological and physical sciences and technology over the roughly 400 years of modern science. I personally have no quarrel with it. It is its adaptation by the social sciences that I, along with many postmodern social science and cultural studies theorists, find problematic. The human–social world, it is argued, cannot be known in the same way as we can know the physical world, because it and our relationship to it (as both its subject and object) are fundamentally different (see, for example, Gergen, 1982, 1994; Kvale, 1992; Newman & Holzman, 1996, 1997; Polkinghorne, 1983; Shotter, 1993a, 1993b). This skepticism toward a natural science approach to human–social phenomena is characteristic of many critical analyses of social science and education. It is a prime motivation for the varied voices within the contemporary postmodern dialogue.

One of the strongest voices to challenge modern epistemology and its ancient Greek roots is *social constructionism*. Its concerns are of a more general nature than either radical–critical pedagogy or sociocultural psychology, dealing as it does with the way all reality, including what are taken to be scientific truths, objective facts, and so on are socially constructed. Going farther than critiques that assert that what is taken as true or superior in a given culture or among a particular grouping is an outgrowth of social process and no more than ideology, a story or a text, social constructionists focus on the human agents in this social process. After all, it is people who create texts, stories, discourses, narratives, and meaning. How meaning is created and used within social relationships is a primary concern of social constructionists.

This contemporary assault on the modern conception of knowledge is directly related to the overidentification of learning with knowing that we have been working to deconstruct. Although the foundational social constructionist literature does not focus on educational theory or practice, it nevertheless poses a powerful challenge to scientific psychology's construction/conception of learning and learners. Moreover, there are social constructionist writings on educational issues that are well grounded in these foundational concerns (see, e.g., Perkinson, 1993; Peters, 1995; Slattery, 1995; Watt, 1994). And finally, the social constructionist assertion that all human experience and action is relational represents a serious (if not entirely successful) attempt to break with particulars, identity, and individual–social duality (Newman & Holzman, 1997).

The recognition that human beings construct meanings—that meaning exists neither out there in the world nor "in our heads"—has profound implications for how psychology, educational research, and schooling practices are done. One of the leading social constructionists, Kenneth Gergen (1994), made an especially clear statement about why meanings and language (and what we understand them to be) are of such importance, as he considers the functions typically attributed to language:

> Can language bear the ponderous responsibility of "depicting" or "mirroring" what is the case? Can we be certain that language is the sort of vehicle that can "convey" truth to others? … On what grounds do we rest such beliefs? Doubt begins when we consider everyday descriptions of people. We describe them as "intelligent," "warm," or "depressed," while their bodies are in a state of continuous motion. Their actions are protean, elastic, ever shifting, and yet our descriptions remain static and frozen. In what sense, then, is language *depicting* their actions? (p. 31)

It is not only in everyday life that we (human beings) generate the conventions of language; the discourses of professionals share the same problems. Psychologists of nearly all persuasions—from psychoanalysts to behaviorists—apply a restricted vocabulary of description "to an unusual and everchanging array of actions" (Gergen, 1994, p. 31). Key to the social constructionist endeavor is the promise that exists in the fundamentally relational nature of language. If any transformation in our understanding and use of language is to take place, it will occur through the conjoint, relational actions of people. For Gergen, a social constructionist approach to human–social phenomena provides three important methodological innovations:

> deconstruction, wherein all presumptions of the true, the rational, and the good are open to suspicion—including those of the suspicious; democratization, wherein the range of voices participating in the consequential dialogues of the science is expanded; and reconstruction, wherein new realities and practices are fashioned for cultural transformation. (Gergen, 1994, pp. 62–63)

Gergen recommended that a relational perspective has much to offer critical theorists, feminists, and others whose critiques tend to be more ideological and political than methodological. In a subsequent paper, Gergen (1995) pointed out how these critiques and the closely related identity politics (social movements centered around gaining rights based on group identity) often perpetuate the very epistemology they are against, by adhering to its methodological presuppositions such as individualism (the particular) and essentialism. Thus, in identity politics discourse, the group has replaced the individual as the center of concern, yet the subtext of individuality remains intact. As Gergen stated, "The group is treated in much the same way discursively as the individual: imbued with good and evil intent, held blameworthy, deemed worthy of rights, and so on. In spite of the shift toward the social, we thus inherit the problems of individualism yet once again—simply one step removed ... we have a battlefield of antagonistic groups" (p. 14).

Gergen further argued that politics and theoretical critique based on identity contain an appeal to essentialism. Making claims for the rights of, for example, women, Blacks, Native Americans, the poor, lesbians, and gay men, on the basis of particular group membership implies an essential entity in that the group name comes to be treated as referential and as if it derived its characteristics from nature. The fact is, of course, that nothing in nature requires it. Gergen then offered a way to move forward. He urged that identity politics transform into *relational politics*, "a politics in which neither self nor other, we nor they, take precedence, but in which relational process serves as the generative source of change" (p. 13).

Gergen's distinction is applicable to psychology and the study of human–social phenomena in general. Identity is the overly psychologized 20th century's *particular* (Newman & Holzman, 1997). Both orthodox, scientific psychology and new psychologies based on group identity, such as Black psychology, feminist psychology, and lesbian and gay psychology, presuppose particularity. They are, to paraphrase Gergen, instances of *identity psychology*. Despite the value of varied critiques of psychology that expose its Eurocentrism, racism, sexism, classism, and homophobia, they are themselves made from an identity perspective. The social constructionist break with identity (particularity) represents an important step away from modern epistemology and scientific psychology and toward an approach to understanding human life not dependent on knowing (Newman & Holzman, 1997).

In the following chapter we revisit the ideas of Vygotsky, this time seeking to discover some things about the revolutionary methodologist rather than the traditional psychologist. It is his work, seen from a social constructionist, postmodern, developmental perspective—a community-building social location and a revolutionary vantage point—that has contributed most powerfully to the creation of the cultural, performatory approach known as developmental learning and that has much to offer in the difficult task of creating schools for growth.

Chapter 3

Vygotsky's Promise: The Unity Learning–Leading–Development

♦ ♦ ♦

Educators and psychologists alike pay lip service to the interrelatedness of learning and development (whatever they might think the connection is). Yet we have seen that the claims psychologists and educators make about learning and development are based on investigative practices that presume their separateness, not only from each other but from much else. Why else would there be attempts to show they are related, to "bring them together?" Why else would questions like, "What are the effects of cognitive development on learning?"; "How does the environment influence learning ability?"; "What role does memory play in learning?" and so on, be asked?

VYGOTSKY'S METHOD

Lev Vygotsky struggled with these kinds of foundational issues. Substantively, he rejected an interactionist (which is really dualistic) view of learning and development. Methodologically, he went a long way toward rejecting the whole of dualistic and reductionistic science and its logic of the particular, even as this paradigm was fast becoming solidified in the field of psychology. His life's work was investigating the very nature of psychology as a science. To Vygotsky, the science activity, like all human activity, embodies its own paradox—it must create its object of investigation. Here is how he put it:

> The search for method becomes one of the most important problems of the entire enterprise of understanding the uniquely human forms of psychological activity. In this case, the method is simultaneously prerequisite and product, the tool and the result of the study. (1978, p. 65)

Vygotsky is offering a new conception of methodology here. In traditional scientific and philosophical terms, method is something separate from the substance and results of an inquiry. It is something to be applied to objects (particulars) in order to yield results. It is, in these ways, instrumental and pragmatic, a functional means to an end. Playing with Vygotsky's language, we can say that traditional method is not "simultaneously ... the tool and the result" but rather *tool for result* (Newman & Holzman, 1993). Of course, this dualistic conception of method presupposes the theory of knowledge we have been discussing, one that requires on the one hand objects of knowledge and, on the other hand, tools (method) for attaining knowledge about the objects.

Vygotsky's method (including his understanding of method) is dialectical rather than dualistic. It is activity-based rather than knowledge/epistemology-based. As "simultaneously tool-and-result," method is practiced, not applied. Knowledge is not separate from the activity of *practicing method*; it is not "out there" waiting to be discovered through the use of an already made tool. According to Vygotsky, practice does not derive from theory. Rather, it is practice that restructures science "from beginning to end," that "poses the task and is the supreme judge of theory" (1982, pp. 388–389). *Practicing method* creates the object of knowledge simultaneously with creating the tool by which that knowledge might be known. Tool-and-result come into existence together; their relationship is one of *dialectical unity*, rather than instrumental duality. Practicing method, then, is carrying out tool-and-result methodology, whereas applying method is carrying out tool for result methodology (see Newman & Holzman, 1993, 1996 for further discussion of these methodologies).

In putting forth this new understanding of method, Vygotsky made a significant break with the dualism, instrumentalism, and reductionism of the dominant scientific paradigm. He planted the seeds of a new psychology, one without a sharp distinction between what psychology is "about" (its substance) and how it is done (its method, or what is sometimes called metapsychology). He engaged in psychological investigation in the interest of discovering/creating what psychology is.

Not everyone sees Vygotsky is these revolutionary terms. Many, if not most, contemporary followers of Vygotsky (including those discussed in chapter 2) ignore his methodological breakthrough, his dialectics, his revolutionariness—all embodied in "tool-and-result." They regard him primarily as a psychologist, specifically an educational or cognitive psychologist whose work has great potential to advance current psychological research about learning. Although the work produced from this perspective has, to some extent, freed psychologists from the knowing mind of the isolated individual as *the* unit of analysis for developmental and educational psychology, I think there are problems with taking Vygotsky in this direction. First, minimizing or ignoring his interest in development leads to a narrow and often distortive reading of his findings. Second, placing Vygotsky within the existing psychological paradigm ignores the importance of his metapsychological mission in favor of his empirical work. He repeatedly spoke of his desire to "find out how science has to be built" (1978, p. 8), the necessity of investigating "the philosophy of the fact" (1987, p. 55), and, as already cited, creating "the search for method."

Further, this reformist "spin" on Vygotsky assumes that psychology's subject matter and paradigm have already been established. The scientific task, then, becomes one of advancing, deepening, refining, and reforming it. This way of looking at psychology and at Vygotsky is not only myopic (the field of psychology is clearly in crisis; there is intense debate and dialogue about its subject matter, paradigm, relevance, validity, and status). It also violates Vygotsky's revolutionary enterprise (Bruner, 1996; Holzman, 1982, 1995a; Newman & Holzman, 1993, 1996; Morss, 1995; Shotter, 1993a, 1993b). I can understand how such a reading of Vygotsky is made—much of his writing concerns topics we identify today with educational or cognitive psychology; he himself was methodologically inconsistent and sometimes made clearly paradigmatic statements. Nevertheless, I think it is a conservative reading that greatly underplays Vygotsky's contribution and potential.

Vygotsky was a leading Marxist theoretician in the early years of the newly formed socialist state, the Soviet Union. Born in 1896 (the same year as Jean Piaget), Vygotsky lived only 38 years as he was seriously ill with tuberculosis during his adult life. Nevertheless, he was amazingly prolific. At last count there were nearly 200 articles, speeches, lectures, and book-length manuscripts on a wide range of topics, including language, learning and development, school instruction, poetry, literature, theater, artistic creativity and imagination, children's play and drawing, written language, memory, emotions, mental retardation, deafness, and blindness. Many of these remain unpublished even in his native Russian, although the last decade's revival of interest in (and commodification of) Vygotsky has resulted in previously unpublished work appearing regularly in Russian, English, and other languages.[1]

Biographical information is relatively sparse and tends to be apocryphal (e.g., as noted by van der Veer & Valsiner, 1991). The Soviet tendency to monumentalize its leaders, the Russian tradition of immortalizing intellectual and cultural figures, coupled with the American zeal for Vygotsky's sociocultural orientation—and, equally, an eagerness to Americanize it—no doubt all contributed to Vygotsky's current "star status." His work and life, however, merit serious deconstructive analysis, some of which is to

---

[1]The most recent compilation of Vygotsky's previously unpublished work is to be found in van der Veer and Valsiner (1994), *The Vygotsky Reader.*

be found in recent publications. (See, e.g., Blanck, 1990; Joravsky, 1989; Kozulin, 1990; Newman & Holzman, 1993; Vygodskaya, 1996. The latter is one of several brief memoirs written by Vygotsky's daughter, herself a psychologist who followed in her father's footsteps.)

Vygotsky's leadership in restructuring psychology, education, and culture in the service of what was hoped would be a new kind of society was abruptly halted. The brief and exhilarating period of experimentation in all forms of life that began in 1917 was stopped when Stalin came to power (Friedman, 1990; Joravsky, 1989; Newman & Holzman, 1993; van der Veer & Valsiner, 1991). Although Vygotsky died in 1934, he was nevertheless a victim of Stalinist repression. His work came under severe attack from academicians/ideologues during the last years of his life and was suppressed after his death. His publications were withdrawn from libraries and universities and only the efforts of a small group of his followers have kept his writings intact and his work alive (Vygodskaya, 1996).

Hardly dogmatic, Vygotsky carefully scrutinized Western and Marxist psychological and philosophical thought (he was well read in both European and American writings) in his efforts to create a new psychology—a science that would shed light on the historical development of human beings and human culture and, simultaneously, address the many difficult challenges presented by the new socialist state. It was this ambition that led to his lifelong concern with the relationship between learning and development. He and his colleagues conducted empirical studies addressing such practical issues as the cultural differences among the hundreds of ethnic groups that formed the new nation, the absence of services for those unable to participate fully in the formation of the new society, the nearly universal illiteracy, and the problem of millions of abandoned and homeless children who roamed the country. In carrying out this work, only rarely did Vygotsky lose sight of the science activity in which he was engaged—the search for method.

In his best known works, *Thinking and Speech* (1987)[2] and *Mind in Society* (1978), we are drawn into a wide-ranging conversation about psychological and educational theory and practice and their philosophical assumptions. As Vygotsky describes and analyzes the work of his contemporaries, he shows us how their (and perhaps our) way of looking at things prevents us from seeing the continuously emergent totality of human psychological activity. He provides a new way of seeing.

Vygotsky's concern with learning and development both informed and was informed by investigations of specific psychological processes presumed in instructional practices designed for the learning of scientific concepts, foreign languages, speaking, writing, and concept formation. He identified

---

[2]Prior English editions of this work published in 1962 and 1986 were entitled *Thought and Language*.

the perspectives on learning/instruction[3] and development that were dominant in his day (and, to a great extent, continue to be in ours) by grouping
them into three categories based on their main assumptions.

The separatist view maintains that instruction/learning and development
are two distinct and essentially independent processes, with development
internal and subordinate to natural laws (Vygotsky, 1987, p. 194) and
instruction an external process that makes use of the potentials of development. The separatist assumption can lead in several directions, Vygotsky
noted. One is toward investigations that attempt to isolate manifestations
of development from manifestations of learning. Vygotsky wryly noted that
the utter failure of this approach has not led investigators to abandon their
method but rather to generate claims at greater and greater levels of
abstraction (as, e.g., in the concept of "pure" development). An extreme
version of the separatist perspective holds that development is everything;
therefore, normal development will occur without any instruction.

Vygotsky (1987) described the more interesting and more common
direction in which the separatist perspective takes us—to the claim that
development is the foundation upon which learning occurs, that learning
"rides on the tail of development" (p. 195). A one-sided dependency
relationship is assumed, whereby instruction and learning depend upon
development but development is unaffected by learning (which is identified
as the fruits of instruction). To illustrate educational practice based in this
one-directional dependency relationship, Vygotsky (1987) listed the kind
of abstract determinations that are made to decide if a child is ready to learn
to write:

> Instruction ... can begin if the child's memory has reached a level of development
> that makes it possible for him to remember the letters of the alphabet, if his attention
> has developed to the extent that it can be maintained on matters of little interest to
> him for a given period of time, and if his thinking has matured to the point that makes
> it possible for him to understand the relationships between sounds and the written
> signs that symbolize them. (p. 195)

Significantly—from the point of view of method—Vygotsky took issue with
the inner–outer duality of this way of conceptualizing the relationship
between learning/instruction and development. As he stated, "Any inter-
penetration or interconnection between these processes is excluded" (p.
195). Development is understood as an internal process; only when certain
cycles or stages of development are completed or bear certain fruits does

---

[3]Vygotsky used the Russian word *obuchenie*, which refers to both teaching and learning. Since the
1978 publication of *Mind in Society* (Cole et al.'s collection of some of Vygotsky's writings), the
convention is to speak of the relationship between learning and development. However, in the 1987
edition of *Thinking and Speech* (from which I quote extensively), Minick used the terms *instruction* and
development rather than *learning* and *development*.

instruction (which is external) become possible. Vygotsky conceded that, in certain cases, some minimum amount of development is necessary for instruction; he also cautioned that focusing on dependency as the primary characteristic of learning/instruction and development leads to significant misunderstandings. The most serious mistake is assuming that learning and instruction have no significance for development. Harking back to the child learning to write, Vygotsky commented that according to this view, "Nothing new emerges in the child's mental development when we teach him to write. The child we have when we finish is identical to the one we had when we began, with the sole exception that he is literate" (p. 196).

Vygotsky reserved his most severe criticism for Piaget, who "pushes this perspective to its logical limit" (p. 196). Vygotsky continued:

> For Piaget, the index of the level of the child's thinking is to be found not in what the child knows or what he is able to learn but in his capacity for thinking in a domain where he has no knowledge. Here, instruction and development or knowledge and thinking are placed in the sharpest possible opposition. (p. 196)

Piaget's mode of investigation, the clinical interview, was based on this opposition. He devised many clever ways to examine children's reasoning in areas where they (supposedly) had no knowledge in order that his results not be contaminated by instruction or what they had learned. He aimed to discover the "pure" development of children's thinking—the inevitable stages and phases that occur regardless of instruction.

Vygotsky's critique of Piaget helps us to see how the dichotomies perpetuated by educational and developmental psychology were produced. The acceptance of Piaget's stages of development is, after all, simultaneously a *rejection* of the significance of learning/instruction for development. Moreover, as Vygotsky pointed out in the previous statement, Piaget insisted that development has to do with thinking (reasoning) whereas learning has to do with knowing (i.e., specific information). Thus, further reductionism and dualism are built into investigative practices, knowledge claims, and instructional techniques. At the research level, there emerged the area of cognitive development as distinct from (in some universities they are literally in separate departments) "the psychology of learning." For all of Piaget's lack of interest in learning, his work helped to construct a conception of learning that is overidentified with the acquisition of knowledge.

For Vygotsky, the identity perspective—that learning/instruction and development are essentially the same—was most closely associated with behaviorism. Here the development of children's thinking is understood as simply the sequential and gradual accumulation of conditioned reflexes (as in the quantitative psychology of learning, whose major proselytizer was the American psychologist Edward Thorndike). Children develop to the extent that they are taught/they learn. Vygotsky discarded this perspective as clearly false, but made note of the fact that it shares the methodological problem of dualism with its diametric opposite, the separatist perspective. One theory "unties the knot" (the relationship between learning/instruction and development); the other "avoids the knot entirely" (p. 196). Both the separatist and the identity perspectives reject unity. Both preclude exploration of the knot; they are dead ends.

Perhaps the solution lies in postulating some sort of middle ground between these two extremes? No. Such an interactionist perspective (the third type Vygotsky discussed) has an inherent duality (p. 197). It accepts the two perspectives and attempts to unify them, but unifying two theories is far from equivalent to taking development and learning/instruction as *a unified process*. Vygotsky analyzes an interesting example of this interactionist perspective—the theory of Koffka (a well-known German contemporary). Although Vygotsky criticized Koffka for his vagueness (Koffka claimed that development and learning mutually influence each other but did not specify how) and his dualism (Koffka divided development into two types—development as maturation, and development that occurs through the influence of instruction)—he also found something new and important in the German psychologist's work. Koffka suggested that learning/instruction can sometimes have developmental consequences that are not immediately obvious, that is, it can produce structural change. To Vygotsky, this made Koffka's theory significantly different from the other perspectives and pointed in the direction he himself was to take. Vygotsky (1987) commented that "Instruction is not limited to trailing after development or moving stride for stride along with it. It can move ahead of development, pushing it further and eliciting new formations" (p. 198).

Vygotsky went on to develop this notion substantively and methodologically (dialectically). His descriptions of the empirical studies he and colleagues conducted alongside the ongoing development of his methodology make fascinating reading (see Vygotsky, 1987, especially chapter 6, pp. 167–242), but are too complex to do justice to here. Instead, I focus on the conceptual and methodological breakthroughs. In rejecting the three perspectives just presented, Vygotsky rejected more than a linear conception of progress; he also rejected a dynamic conception of process. What he offered in their stead is a *dialectical conception of activity*.

In doing so, Vygotsky brought to psychology a new conceptual tool—Marx's dialectical historical materialism—and introduced to psychology a new conception of change—change as qualitative transformation *of totalities*. He was not merely identifying another way that learning/instruction and development are "related." Rather, he introduced to psychology a new conception of relationship itself, one not premised on *particulars* but on *totality*. To Vygotsky, learning/instruction and development are *a dialectical unity in which learning leads development*. What is a dialectical unity? What is meant by "leads?" Exploring these questions will help us understand qualitative transformation, the Marxian–Vygotskian concept of activity, and development as continuously emergent, relational human activity.

Recall Vygotsky's characterization of the search for method as "tool-and-result." This is a methodological claim, for he is positing a relationship of dialectical unity (activistic inseparability), not a relationship of cause or precondition. Neither tool nor result is the cause of, nor comes before, the other; neither is comprehensible apart from the other. They come into existence together, influencing each other in complex and changing ways as the totality tool-and-result develops. Vygotsky wanted us to see the totality, the whole, the unity, tool-and-result, because it is only from that vantage point that we can come to understand anything about its processes and functioning. Seeing particulars, seeing parts as making up the whole—rather than seeing the whole and the interrelationships within it—we neither see nor understand very much. His rejection of particulars (and reductionist methodology) is clear in statements such as the following:

> … the development of each mental function depends on … changes in interfunctional relationships. Consciousness develops as a whole…. Development is not a sum of the changes occurring in each of the separate functions. Rather, the fate of each functional part of consciousness depends on changes in the whole. (1987, pp. 187–188)

The dialectical unity learning/instruction–leading–development develops as a whole. Learning cannot exist without development and development cannot exist without learning. One is not the cause of the other; rather, they are historical biconditions within the ever-evolving totality. But, you might be asking, if one is not the cause or precondition of the other, how can Vygotsky say that learning *leads* development? Doesn't "leads" imply "cause," or at least "coming before?" What else could he mean when he says that learning is "ahead of" and "in advance of" development? Or that "Instruction would be completely unnecessary if it merely utilized what had already matured in the developmental process, if it were not itself a source of development" (1987, p. 212).

Herein lies what is most fascinating and revolutionary (and philosophical) about Vygotsky's discovery that learning leads development. For our ordinary language use, which is exceedingly nondialectical, does suggest that "lead" connotes chronology, linearity, hierarchy, or cause, as in "One thing leads to another"; "She led me to the house I was looking for"; "The United States leads the world in …"; and "Reading that book led me to pursue a career in astronomy." And indeed, many followers of Vygotsky understand learning–leads–development to mean that learning precedes and/or causes development. In my opinion, such a reading is misguided. For it would simply be the negation of the widely held view that development leads (in linear, chronological, and/or causal fashion) learning, and would thus discount his rejection of the causal–linear model of human development on which both positions are based. Moreover, it denies the totality of Vygotsky's enterprise in which dialectical unity rather than metaphysical duality was central (Newman & Holzman, 1993).

My understanding of Vygotsky's meaning draws on another of his provocative and revolutionary methodological claims—the notion of *completion*. Vygotsky introduced this conception as a challenge to the traditional ways of understanding language (speaking) and its relationship to thought (thinking), namely, that when we speak we are *expressing* our thoughts. Not so for Vygotsky:

> The structure of speech is not simply the mirror image of the structure of thought. It cannot, therefore, be placed on thought like clothes off a rack. Speech does not merely serve as the expression of developed thought. Thought is restructured as it is transformed into speech. It is not expressed but completed in the word. Therefore, precisely because of the contrasting directions of the movement, the development of the internal and external aspects of speech form a true unity. (1978, p. 251)

Saving further exploration of the implications of a completive relation between speaking and thinking for later in the chapter, I here only characterize the unity relationship learning–leading–development as one of completion. Learning "completes" development, while development "completes" learning although, of course, they do not complete each other in the same way, since learning leads development (see Newman & Holzman, 1993, for further discussion).

THE ZONE OF PROXIMAL DEVELOPMENT IS NOT A ZONE

How learning/instruction and development complete each other becomes understandable with the introduction of what is perhaps Vygotsky's most well-known conceptual and methodological discovery—*the zone of proximal development*. The nearest thing to a definition of the ZPD Vygotsky offered is the oft-quoted:

> Every function in the child's cultural development appears twice: first on the social level and later, on the individual level; first, *between* people (*interpsychological*), and then *inside* the child (*intrapsychological*). This applies equally to all voluntary attention, to logical memory, and to the formation of concepts. All the higher mental functions originate as actual relations between people. (1978, p. 57)

Vygotsky thus drew attention to the participatory nature of ongoing development and the social–cultural–historical nature of forms of human activity. Many psychologists and educators have understood this statement instrumentally and dualistically. Unintentionally or not, they utilize a particularistic ontology (presuming a separation between individual and society) and perpetuate an essentially interactionist position on learning/instruction and development. They take the ZPD—the difference between what one can do "with others" and what one can do "by oneself"—to be a tool (for result) for understanding individual mental processes.

In a typical research study, a dyad (e.g., a mother and child or two children) are observed doing some task (as defined by the researchers). Of interest is how the "novice"—the one who is less developed or less knowledgeable—learns from the "expert." Learning is still understood to be what the individual does. The *joint activity* of the dyad (the things they do and say) is reduced to the means by which learning is accomplished. We saw an instance of this research approach in Wertsch's puzzle completion task discussed in chapter 2. The ZPD is thus turned into a principle for accounting for how a person ever learns anything—given that he or she is fundamentally an individual. Premised on the dualistic and particularistic separation of individual and society, it is an attempt to "reunite" them. (See Newman & Holzman, 1993, for an extensive discussion of such contemporary studies.)

What happens if we try to follow Vygotsky's dialectical tool-and-result methodology? What if we begin with the totality individual-and-society? Might we see the ZPD not as an instrumental tool but as developmental activity itself? From the revolutionary vantage point (that is, the creating of a new psychology), the ZPD looks very different. It is not a zone at all, but the "life space" in which the so-called higher psychological processes in which human beings engage (such as speaking, thinking, and problem solving) emerge and develop. The critical feature of the ZPD as life space is that it is *inseparable from the we who produce it*. It is and is produced through tool-and-result methodology—the relational activity of human beings creating their lives:

> It is the socially–historically–culturally produced environment in which and how human beings organize and reorganize their relationships to each other and to nature, that is, the elements of social life. It is where human beings—determined, to be sure, by sometimes empirically observable circumstances—totally transform these very circumstances (making something new); it is the "location" of human (revolutionary) activity. (Newman & Holzman, 1996, p. 180)

Whereas most of Vygotsky's investigation of the ZPD concerns learning and instruction in schools, it is his analysis of the ZPD of the language-learning young child that I find most suggestive of the unique revolutionary character of human growth, as in the following description (originally published in 1935):

> We have a child who has only just begun to speak and he pronounces single words, as children who are just mastering the art of speech tend to do. But is fully developed speech, which the child is only able to master at the end of this period of development,

already present in the child's environment? It is, indeed. The child speaks in one word phrases, but his mother talks to him in language which is already grammatically and syntactically formed and which has a large vocabulary, even though it is being toned down for the child's benefit. All the same, she speaks using the fully perfected form of speech. Let us agree to call this developed form, which is supposed to make its appearance at the end of the child's development, the final or ideal form (as it is called in contemporary paedology)—ideal in the sense that it acts as a model for that which should be achieved at the end of the developmental period; and final in the sense that it represents what the child is supposed to attain at the end of his development. And let us call the child's form of speech the primary or rudimentary form. The greatest characteristic feature of child development is that this development is achieved under particular conditions of interaction with the environment, where this ideal and final form (that form which is going to appear only at the end of the process of development) is not only already there in the environment and from the very start in contact with the child, but actually interacts and exerts a real influence on the primary form, on the first steps of the child's development. *Something which is only supposed to take shape at the very end of development, somehow influences the very first steps in this development.* (1994, p. 348)

What point is Vygotsky making here? What can he possibly mean by insisting that the developed form "is already there?" What "there" is he talking about? It clearly is not there "in the child" and it clearly is there "in the mother." So it being "already there" in the mother is a trivial point. Such a particularistic and dualistic reading would be silly. The only way to make sense of Vygotsky's description of the coming-to-be-a-speaker child is to abandon the notion of particularity, in this case, the particular point of origin (the mother) to define what was "already there." For to retain it would be to insist that developed language has a starting point, a beginning, a location (from which it follows that it is dualistically divided from "what follows"), thereby rendering Vygotsky's argument meaningless.[4] Rather, we need to evaluate his argument from the point of view of the ever-changing totality individual-and-society or total environment (i.e., the "existing" environment and the environment-being-created). Both developed language and rudimentary language are present in the total environment. The total environment includes both child and mother—not as particulars that make up the whole or that exist within the bounds of the environment—but *as inseparable from and creators of it*. The point is that people are no more "in" environments in the sense of being included in them than noodles are "in" noodle soup. (It would be strange indeed to declare that "noodles are included in noodle soup.") The total environment is not a place but an activity.

---

[4]The fact that in this very quote Vygotsky speaks of beginning and end points poses a problem for my argument only if we read Vygotsky particularistically and piecemeal. Shaped by the scientific and philosophical paradigms of modernism, of both the bourgeois and Marxist varieties, his language and conceptions were, lawfully, modernist and his formulations not consistently dialectical and relational. Nevertheless, I think an accounting of his position has to be made from the perspective of the totality of his work and the task that he tells us he set himself.

In fact, Vygotsky's point is far from trivial. I think he has, if not fully identified, then at least pointed the way to the paradoxical nature of human activity. We all live simultaneously in society and in history, more precisely in the dialectical unity society/history. We develop our lives through adapting societally (i.e., to society—the name we give to specific temporal and spatial "locations") and at the same time adapting historically (engaging in the revolutionary activity of transforming these societal circumstances). If we stop adapting to history, we not only stop developing, we eventually stop adapting to society (Newman & Holzman, 1993).

In society (most, if not all, of them) there are beginnings and endings, but "in history" there are none. This "dual location" that is the human condition produces the following paradox. In the ZPD (the dialectical unity society/history) where learning leads development (another dialectical unity), it is development that "comes first" (in the societal sense of being temporally prior). Perhaps learning is then the discovery of what was "already there." In order to understand understanding activistically (nonepistemologically), perhaps we need to give up origins and "challenge the direction (the flow) of time itself.... What we know is what we had to know (had to have known) in order to have had the developmental relational experience of constructive discovery" (Newman & Holzman, 1996, pp. 40–41).

The continuous shaping and reshaping of what Vygotsky calls the "rudimentary" and "developed" forms of speech through joint activity (adapting to society/history) simultaneously *is and creates* the ZPD. It is in the "language-games" (to be discussed in chapter 4) that very young children and their caregivers create that we can see how learning leads development. Here is a typical example of a ZPD-creating language-game played by a 21-month-old boy and an adult taken from Bloom, Hood, and Lightbown (1974, p. 380):

Child: (opening cover of tape recorder) open/open/open
Adult: did you open it?
Child: (watching tape recorder) open it
Adult: did you open the tape recorder?
Child: (watching tape recorder) tape recorder.

The babbling baby's rudimentary speech is a *creative imitation* of the more developed speaker. It is not, Vygotsky warns us, to be understood as the kind of mimicry that some parrots and monkeys do. It is creative, relational revolutionary activity. It is what makes it possible for the child to do what she or he is not yet capable of or, in Vygotsky's words, "to be a head taller than [she or] he is" (Vygotsky, 1978, p. 102). In imitating in the linguistic ZPD, the child is *performing* (beyond him or herself) as a speaker.

Performance is, however, not a "solo act." In the linguistic ZPD, the more developed speaker *completes* the child in the sense that, as we saw earlier, Vygotsky viewed speaking as completing (not expressing) thinking. Mothers, fathers, grandparents, siblings, and others immediately accept infants into the community of speakers. As Vygotsky made clear in the lengthy description just given, and as the preceding example illustrates, more experienced speakers neither tell infants that they are too young, give them a grammar book and dictionary to study, correct them, nor remain silent around them. Rather, they relate to infants and babies as capable of far more than they could possibly do; they relate to them as beyond themselves, as speakers, feelers, thinkers, and makers of meaning.

Creative imitation and *completion* are the dominant activities in the ZPD. They are the relational activities that produce the environment in which learning leads development and the learning that leads development *simultaneously*. Their "product" is nothing less than a new total environment of speakers. The significance of the ZPD as creative activity is that the capacity to speak and to make meaning is inextricably connected to transforming the total environment of speakers.

The lesson I take from Vygotsky is this: A total environment in which very young children are related to by themselves and others (a relational activity) as communicative social beings is *how they get to be so*. They say things—they babble, make sounds, use words, make meaning—as an inseparable part of participating in social life. And they participate fully—before they know the rules of how to participate. Indeed, it is only by playing the game that they eventually learn the rules. In my view, Vygotsky identified perhaps the most important of all human activities—our capacity to relate to ourselves and others as *other than, and in advance of, our development*. This is how, in the dialectical unity learning–leading–development, learning and development complete each other, and how development "is already present in the child's environment."

Chapter 4

Performing Development:
Nonepistemological Learning

◆ ◆ ◆

If we take seriously Vygotsky's revolutionary conception—that learning and development are a dialectical unity in which learning leads (in nonlinear fashion) development—we should be deeply unsettled. I know I am. Having considered the philosophical, pedagogical, and political implications of Vygotsky's work, I have experienced something akin to the "ontological insecurity" first described by the anti-psychiatrist R. D. Laing (1959). The revolutionary Vygotsky challenges our assumptions about what makes us human, how we relate to the world, what it means to act, think, feel, speak, and relate to one another. He uproots our species identity. We human beings are not, as we had thought, primarily conceivers and perceivers, but producers, builders, and creators of our collective lives.

Our "competitive edge" over other species these thousands of years is not our seemingly unlimited skill in the instrumental use of tools, but our remarkable capacity to reshape the totality of our existence, that is, to *make tools* of a very special kind—ones that are, in Vygotsky's words, "simultaneously the tool and the result." Those of us who are psychologists or educators should not be primarily observers, analysts, interpreters, explainers, and critics as we were trained to be, but revolutionary activists collectively engaged in what Vygotsky called the ongoing "search for method." We have to create our object of study even as we study it, he tells us (in a methodologically sophisticated practical–critical specification of Marx's *XI Thesis on Feuerbach*, "The philosophers have only *interpreted* the world, in various ways; the point is to *change* it (Marx, 1973, p. 123).

If this is not mere rhetoric, then what is the new practice we need to be engaging in? Is it possible to create development in a culture so foundationally antidevelopmental? What do we create it out of? If these questions themselves are not just rhetoric, then it would seem to be equally important to know how I have come to ask them. We would need to examine the social–cultural–historical community of practice in which my revolutionary reading of Vygotsky has occurred.

In chapter 1, I termed our community of practice *a developing development community*. This new *kind of* community is Vygotskian in its tool-and-result character, for it supports developmental activity and, at the same time, its noninstrumental, nonpragmatic (tool-and-result) activity is "merely" the developmental activity it supports (not some other outcome or product). It is within the activity of this community that Vygotsky most fully breaks with scientific psychology and its philosophical presuppositions. I put forth in this chapter the critical features of the new activity–theoretic, social constructionist practice of developmental learning, and attempt to show how this activity is not one of applying Vygotsky instrumentally to specific areas such as education and therapy, but rather one of transforming his work via a nonepistemological, therapeutic tool-and-result modality.

A nonepistemological, therapeutic modality might seem to be a contradiction in terms, given how thoroughly cognitized psychotherapy and other approaches to human subjectivity, including psychology and psychiatry, have become. Whether approaches to (what is referred to as) psychopathology or mental illness are proclaimed to be helping, curing, healing, or merely the relieving of symptoms, they are nearly all based in cognitions (accountings, appraisals, understandings, and interpretations that take the form of diagnoses, labels, and identities).

Treatment has been shaped by the modern epistemological paradigm (knowing). To wit: To understand something is to *know something about* something else. In the case of human emotions, the "something else" typically takes one or another of the following forms: aggregated data concerning behaviors classified as either normal or abnormal; facts or memories about a person's childhood; a detailed family history; quantitative data on brain functioning. The pseudoscientific nature of these cognitively based methods of accounting—classification, interpretation, and explanation—has been written about extensively (e.g., Dawes, 1994; Ingleby, 1980; Newman & Holzman, 1996; Szasz, 1961, 1996; Timpanero, 1985; Torrey, 1992). Yet, despite its highly questionable status as scientific investigation and its documented failure, the so-called objective study of the subjective still reigns supreme.

As noted earlier, the recent postmodern turn within psychology raises doubts about objectivity (not only scientific objectivity but also whether there is an objective reality at all). Equally important are the things it raises about the relevance and validity of a knowing paradigm in relation to human subjectivity, especially emotionality and its institutionalized treatment modality, psychotherapy (McNamee & Gergen, 1993). Perhaps therapeutic understanding is not understanding as we "know" it; perhaps it has nothing to do with science, diagnoses, cognition, mental states, inner realities, or private worlds. Therapists and clients alike acknowledge that merely talking to another person about how one is feeling is helpful. Perhaps it is the relational activity of the therapeutic modality *as activity* that is of value rather than the specific insights, interpretations, or explanations that grow out of the activity. Perhaps it is the talking—not what is talked about—that is therapeutic. Perhaps "knowing emotionally" is not knowing at all (Newman & Holzman, 1996, p. 162; see also Shotter, 1993b).

THE ACTIVITY OF SPEAKING

If anything can be said to have guided the overall therapeutic modality of the developing development community (as well as its specific clinical approach, social therapy), it is this combination of a skepticism toward knowing and an appreciation of the social activity of speaking.

What is the activity of speaking? And why would it be therapeutically helpful? Here, again, Vygotsky unsettles our conventional understanding. In both linguistic and psychological theorizing and everyday thinking on the matter, it is typically said that people are expressing their thoughts, communicating or transmitting information when they speak. However, as seen in chapter 3, Vygotsky's (1987) views on language and thought (speaking and thinking) challenge what is a mentalistic and representationalist conception of language, for he claimed that speaking does not express, but completes, thinking. The relationship between thought and word, he says, "is not a thing but a process, a movement from thought to word and from word to thought.... Thought is not expressed but completed in the word. We can, therefore, speak of the establishment (i.e., the unity of being and nonbeing) of thought in the word" (p. 250).

Speaking/thinking (a dialectical unity) is social–cultural activity. Language is social–cultural activity. Human beings not only use language (a tool for a result); we also make language (a tool-and-result). Vygotsky suggests that it is not language *behavior*, that is, our instrumental use of language to transmit, evaluate, analyze, describe, and interpret, but rather language *activity*—the making of meaning, the completion of thought in the word—that is of developmental significance. This distinction between behavioral use and activity is typically overlooked in neo-Vygotskian studies that focus exclusively on language as a psychological–cultural tool that children learn to use, enabling them to "appropriate the culture" via "mediational means" (see, e.g., Cole, 1995; Lave & Wenger, 1991; Rogoff, 1990; Wertsch, 1991).

In addition to Vygotsky, it is the Austrian-born philosopher Ludwig Wittgenstein whose views on language have so strongly influenced our developmental practice. He was perhaps the most influential, original, and enigmatic philosopher of the 20th century.[1] His writings from 1919 until the 1950s turned Western philosophy upside down. Wittgenstein is typically associated with the mid-20th-century "school" known as analytic philosophy, although other philosophical movements, including those known as ordinary language philosophy and logical positivism, claim him as a major influence.

Contemporary philosophers divide his work into the early and later writings. The early Wittgenstein attempted to solve the problems of philosophy by showing the logical form of language in a manner consistent with what logicians and mathematicians were doing at the time. However, he soon abandoned this approach and devoted the rest of his intellectual life to the exploration/investigation of a nonessentialist philosophy, that is, philosophy without theses or premises, philosophy as method. In an unusual display of intellectual honesty, Wittgenstein pointed to the errors and dogmatism of his own early masterpiece, *Tractatus Logico-Philosophicus*; in the best known of his later writings, *Philosophical Investigations*, he repudiated the "old ways of thinking and "grave mistakes" he had made in that early work (Wittgenstein, 1953, pp. v–vi).

Wittgenstein's writings are more explicitly antireferential and anticognitive than Vygotsky's. His views on philosophy, language, philosophical scientific methodology, and psychology consistently eschew essences, deeper meanings, metaphysics, and underlying rules and patterns. His effort was to create a new nonsystematic, non-truth-based understanding of understanding (which, in effect, would do away with Philosophy with a capital P). In this regard, his work can be seen not merely as critical but also as therapeutic. This has been noted by several contemporary analysts, most eloquently by the leading Wittgensteinian scholar Gordon Baker. According to Baker (1992), we would do well to pay attention to Wittgenstein's "overall therapeutic conception of his philosophical investigations" (p. 129). Rather than advocating a generalized position, Wittgenstein "always sought to address specific philosophical problems of definite individuals" (p. 129). Baker (1992) used a medical analogy to further make his point:

> He [Wittgenstein] did not see himself in the role of a public health official whose brief was to eradicate smallpox from the face of the earth (for example to eliminate Cartesian dualism once for all by means of the Private Language Argument). Rather he operated as a general practitioner who treated the bumps that various individual patients had got by running their heads up against the limits of language. (p. 129)

Others philosophers (e.g., Peterman, 1992) and, more recently, psychologists (Bakhurst, 1991, 1995; Chapman & Dixon, 1987; Gergen & Kaye,

---

[1]Wittgenstein's philosophy has been the subject of thousands of books and articles of commentary, his life the subject of hundreds of biographies and memoirs, films, plays, paintings, music, and works of fiction. Among the best attempts to integrate his life and work are Ray Monk's *Ludwig Wittgenstein: The Duty of Genius* (1990) and Janik and Toulmin's *Wittgenstein's Vienna* (1973).

1993; Jost, 1995; Shotter, 1991, 1993a, 1993b, 1995) approached Wittgenstein from a similar vantage point, finding his writings compatible with their views on the subjective and ethical dimensions of human development. My colleagues in the developing development community and I concur: "[Wittgenstein's] critique took the form of a non-systematic 'client-specific' treatment plan for both philosophers and ordinary people. For Wittgenstein, philosophy is the disease, language the carrier, philosophical scientific methodology the hospital which science neither wants, nor needs. And psychology is the pseudoscientific, bogus cure" (Newman & Holzman, 1996, p. 50).

Language is the carrier of the disease, for Wittgenstein, because of the overdetermining representationalist connection between language and thought we in our culture make (the view that language expresses thought that Vygotsky rejected). We presume that our thoughts, words, and deeds are lawfully connected, and speak of and seek causes, correspondences, parallels, and generalizations between and among things we think, say, and do. Wittgenstein's method is to show us again and again the extent to which our thinking is strongly shaped by assumptions and presuppositions about language that derive from how we have identified it as fundamentally mentalistic. His method of "therapeutic cure" is to exaggerate the normal (and normally unnoticed) process of assuming that language is rule-governed, consistent from one situation to another, denotative, representational, and expressive, and thereby to show the absurdity of such assumptions. This clears up confusions, relieves what he called our "mental cramps," and, hopefully, stops individuals from asking the kinds of questions or thinking the kinds of thoughts that get them into these confusions in the first place. His goal is to help us get on with things, to "move about around things and events in the world instead of trying to delineate their essential features" (van der Merwe & Voestermans, 1995, p. 38).

Interestingly, Wittgenstein's radical challenge to the philosophy of language has suffered a fate similar to the one that overtook Vygotsky's challenge to psychology. Most of Wittgenstein's followers turn what is an activity–theoretic stance toward language into a pragmatic one, just as so many of Vygotsky's followers turned his activity–theoretic stance toward learning and development into a pragmatic one (by seeing language as an instrumental tool that mediates between the individual and the culture). This can be seen most clearly in Wittgenstein's most well-known conception—the language-game. Language-games are a means of clearing away the confusing modes of thought forced upon us by our overly mentalistic understanding of language (again, the conviction that language expresses thought). We make problems (confusions, muddles) for ourselves as we struggle to reconnect the unity thinking/speaking that we have, unwittingly, separated. The language-game—as activity—prevents this muddle:

> I shall in the future again and again draw your attention to what I shall call language-games. These are ways of using signs simpler than those in which we use the signs of our highly complicated everyday language. Language-games are the forms of language with which a child begins to make use of words. The study of language-games is the study of primitive forms of language or primitive languages. If we want to study the problems of truth or falsehood, of the agreement or disagreement of propositions with reality, of the nature of assertion, assumption and question, we shall with great advantage look at primitive forms of language in which these forms of thinking appear without the confusing background of highly complicated processes of thought. When we look at such simple forms of language the mental mist which seems to enshroud our ordinary use of language disappears. We see activities, reactions, which are clear-cut and transparent. (1965, BBB, p. 17)[2]

Wittgenstein never defines language-games, which is not surprising given his aversion to definition. Different language-games, like everything else, bear "family resemblances" to one another. At times, Wittgenstein speaks of language-games in a way that emphasizes their pragmatic function and seems to equate meaning with use rather than with activity, for example, "The meaning of a word is its use in the language" (1953, 43). Although statements such as this strengthen the propensity for philosophers and psychologists to take Wittgenstein's major contributions to be the identification of meaning with use and the language-game as a pragmatic tool of analysis, it is a reading that misses what is most methodologically challenging in his work. Statements like the following: "The term 'language-game' is meant to bring into prominence the fact that the *speaking* of language is part of an activity, or of a form of life" (1953, p. 23); and "Only in the stream of thought and life do words have meaning" (1967, p. 173), where Wittgenstein emphasized the activity of language and the value of language-games in showing this, suggest an activity–theoretic, relational understanding rather than a pragmatic one. I share with others the view that it is language as activity that is central to Wittgenstein's understanding—and to understanding the therapeutic character and developmental contribution of his work (see Baker, 1992; Holzman, 1996; Newman & Holzman, 1996; Shotter, 1993a, 1993b, 1995; van der Merwe & Voestermans, 1995).

Let us look at some examples of Wittgenstein's method. In this first case, he challenged the reader to give up our need for generalization and definition as fundamental for understanding language and meaning:

> 65. For someone might object against me: "You take the easy way out! You talk about all sorts of language-games, but have nowhere said what the essence of a language-game, and hence of language, is: what is common to all these activities, and what makes them into language or parts of language. So you let yourself off the very part of

---

[2]The convention in philosophical literature is to cite Wittgenstein's writings by title (abbreviated) and paragraph or page number. Full titles of abbreviated texts can be found in the references.

the investigation that once gave you yourself most headache, the part about the *general form of propositions* and of language."

And this is true.—Instead of producing something common to all that we call language, I am saying that these phenomena have no one thing in common which makes us use the same word for all,—but that they are *related* to one another in many different ways. And it is because of this relationship, or these relationships, that we call them all "language."

66. ... Don't say: "There *must* be something common, or they would not be called 'games'"—but *look and see* whether there is anything common to all —For if you look at them you will not see something that is common to *all*, but similarities, relationships, and a whole series of them at that. (1953, *PI*, p. 31)

In the next case from his *Remarks on the Philosophy of Psychology*, Wittgenstein (1980) engaged the fundamentality of causality, correspondence, and essences:

905. I saw this man years ago: now I have seen him again, I recognize him, I remember his name. And why does there have to be a cause of this remembering in my nervous system? Why must something or other, whatever it may be, be stored-up there *in any form*? Why must a trace have been left behind? Why should there not be a psychological reality to which *no* physiological regularity corresponds? If this upsets our concepts of causality then it is high time they were upset. [cf. Z, p. 610] (*RPP*, p. 160)

In the next example (part of a long dialogue that concerns solving a number series problem) Wittgenstein deconstructed the picture we have of meaning as lying behind or under the surface:

154. If there has to be anything 'behind the utterance of the formula' it is *particular circumstances*, which justify me in saying I can go on—when the formula occurs to me.

Try not to think of understanding as a 'mental process' at all—For, *that* is the expression which confuses you. But ask yourself: in what sort of case, in what kind of circumstances, do we say, "Now I know how to go on," when, that is, the formula *has* occurred to me?

In the sense in which there are processes (including mental processes) which are characteristic of understanding, understanding is not a mental process. (1953, *PI*, p. 61)

Philosophizing in this way (playing language-games) is a very different practice from learning Philosophy. What is therapeutic about it (i.e., what gets us unstuck so that, in Wittgenstein's words, "now we can go on") is that it keeps us from institutionalizing our words. This kind of unsystematic philosophizing, the continuous playing of Wittgensteinian language-games, helps to challenge the tendency in our culture for language to become reified as a thing-in-itself that is "above us" and "about" us (and comes to define our experiences). It helps us see and do language as a "form of life."

These language-games are ones in which, as we saw in the above excerpts, the dominant feature is the questioning activity. What "makes the mental mist disappear, the problem vanish"—that is, what is therapeutic—is not "the answer" nor even the answering activity, but rather the activity of asking the questions. Asking "big" questions about "little" things—practical philosophizing—can liberate us from reified language use and societally and culturally overdetermined conversations (Newman, 1996). For example, asking an 8-year-old who states emphatically, "I can't spell," "Is 'I can't spell' like 'I can't fly?'" can create an entirely different conversation from the ones that unfold from the more usual responses, such as "Yes, you can" or "Let me teach you." Wittgenstein has said about his own method: "What I do is suggest, or even invent, other ways of looking.... You thought that there was one possibility, or only two at most. But I made you think of others. Furthermore, I made you see that it was absurd to expect the concept to conform to those narrow possibilities ... thus your mental cramp is relieved ..." (cited in Monk, 1990, p. 502).

The concern of our developing development community is how we can further develop from where we are to where we collectively choose to go. Our pedagogy, in this Wittgensteinian sense, is therapeutically developmental and activity-based rather than cognitively and/or morally controlling and epistemologically based. It is a practical synthesis of Vygotsky and Wittgenstein, a synthesis that is rooted in their transformation from a cognitive to a therapeutic modality. From such a therapeutic vantage point, the ZPD is for Vygotsky what *form of life* is for Wittgenstein. A ZPD is a form of life in which people collectively and relationally create developmental learning that goes beyond what any individual in the group could learn on her or his "own." Our effort is to create continuously overlapping ZPDs, a particular relational activity that simultaneously is and makes possible the transforming of rigidified behavior (forms of life that have become alienated and fossilized) into new forms of life (Newman & Holzman, 1996).

PLAY AS AND IN THE ZPD

How is this done? We sometimes describe our developing development community as one in which we play (in Vygotsky's sense) language-games (in Wittgenstein's sense). Vygotsky (1987) believed that "a child's greatest achievements are possible in play" (p. 100) because the kind of free play young children engage in creates a ZPD. Play differs from nonplay (in which learning–leading–development can also occur) in freeing us from situational constraints. According to Vygotsky, the unique feature of free play (the pretend and fantasy activities characteristic of early childhood) is the creation of an imaginary situation in which meaning dominates action:

> Though the play-development relationship can be compared to the instruction-development relationship, play provides a much wider background for changes in needs and consciousness. Action in the imaginative sphere, in an imaginary situation, the creation of voluntary intentions, and the formation of real-life plans and volitional

motives—all appear in play and make it the highest level of preschool development. The child moves forward essentially through play activity. Only in this sense can play be considered a leading activity that determines the child's development. (Vygotsky, 1978, pp. 102–103)

Some followers of Vygotsky have turned "leading activity" into a reified psychological and pedagogical concept. For example, the contemporary Russian psychologists, Davydov and Elkonin, theorize different "leading activities" that correspond to different "stages of development." Play is claimed to be the leading activity of early childhood, learning the leading activity of middle childhood, and social relations the leading activity of adolescence (see Davydov, 1988, 1995; Elkonin & Davydov, 1966). With this stagist view of development, the truly developmental (revolutionary) characteristic of play to which Vygotsky pointed gets reduced to a "social catalyst" for the unfolding of what is "natural" at a certain age. What is missed is the tremendous potential of play for the continuous creation of new forms of life—throughout life.

In contrast, from a social constructionist, therapeutic, developmental learning perspective, the developmental potential of play lies in the fact that it allows us to be more directly the producers of our activity. In everyday life, people are guided—indeed, typically overdetermined—by well-learned perceptual, cognitive, and emotional behaviors. (For many of life's tasks—buying groceries, making a phone call, driving to work—such guidance is fully functional and effective.) When we play, we have more control in producing and organizing these elements, perhaps in new ways. Rather than being guided by rules that have been formulated in advance and to which we have become so well adapted, Vygotsky (1978) said that free play contains rules "that stem from an imaginary situation" (p. 95). That is, the rules of free play create an imaginary situation *even as* they stem from the imaginary situation. They have the critical developmental characteristic of being "tool-and-resultish"—they are incomprehensible apart from the process of their development (Newman & Holzman, 1993, pp. 100–102).

Vygotsky's analysis of play, its role in development, and its transformation through development is, in my opinion, a provocative challenge to the typical instrumental understanding of the significance of play for development. Even those psychologists influenced by Vygotsky are, like their more traditional colleagues, trapped within a cognitive paradigm (e.g., Rogoff, 1990; Rogoff & Lave, 1984; Wertsch, 1985a). For them, the value of play is that it facilitates the learning of social–cultural roles; in other words, it is a tool that serves to mediate between the individual and the culture. Through acting out roles (play-acting), children "try out" the roles they will soon take on in "real life." Certainly, play is commonly put to such important instrumental use. However, this is not what makes play developmental; from an activity–theoretic, therapeutic perspective, play is more tool-and-resultish than that. In my view, free or pretend play is more akin to performing (in

Vygotsky's sense of performing beyond yourself or being a head taller than you are) than to acting:

> When children, for example, play Mommy and Daddy they are least like Mommy and Daddy because Mommy and Daddy are not playing or performing; they are acting out their societally predetermined roles. We are all cast by society into very sharply determined roles; what one does in a role is act it. Performance differs from acting in that it is the socialized activity of people self-consciously creating new roles out of what exists for a social performance. Children playing Mommy and Daddy are not acting but performing—creating new roles for themselves, reorganizing environmental scenes. In this sense, "zpd play" is a history game—the putting together of elements of the social environment in ways which help to see and show meaning-making as creative, productive activity—which produces learning–leading–development. (Newman & Holzman, 1993, pp. 102–103)

DEVELOPING: PERFORMING WHO YOU'RE NOT

Play, understood as performance, is being who you are not. Performance, understood as developmental, is creating who you are by being who you are not. Development, understood as relational activity, involves the continuous creating of stages (ZPDs) on which one performs "oneself" through incorporating "the other." For if human development is to have any meaning—that is, if it is not, ultimately, reducible to learning or maturation or societal adaptation, then must it not have this dialectical, emergent, activistic characteristic? And if human learning is to be of any value (to our species as a whole and to its particular members), then mustn't it be developmental?

An obvious but largely overlooked characteristic of the human species is that we are all performers. From the creatively imitative babble of babies as they learn to talk and the imaginative pretend play of young children being mommy, daddy, Barney, Michael Jackson, and airline pilots, to the creation of countless characters on Broadway and off-Broadway, in opera houses and thousands of comedy clubs, concert halls, and community theaters, people—amateurs and professionals—perform as "other than who we are." Human beings have the capacity to create endless performances of ourselves that, far from being determined by how we feel, our current level of development, or our self-image, are in a certain sense in opposition to or beyond them. Young children and skilled actors are both model performers. Young children simply do not yet know the "right" way to behave; professional actors have been trained to use their creative imagination to go beyond their well-learned nonstage behavior. Although actors might very well feel depressed or angry, they would immediately lose their jobs if they were to get on stage and act depressed or talk about how they were feeling instead of performing their parts in plays or improvisations. Those of us who are not children or skilled actors rarely have the support in our daily lives to exercise this creative aspect of ourselves. Beyond early childhood, we rarely have the support to create our development through performing.

Children learn to talk and use language by performing development. They create who they are by being who they are not. They engage, with others, in the revolutionary activity of making meaning, the taking of elements of their life space and reorganizing them to make something new—a conversation, a language-game, a speaker (Newman & Holzman, 1993). They play, in Vygotsky's sense of play, with language. Using the predetermined tools of language to create something other than what is predetermined, disrupting the existing organization of sound, syntax, and meaning—these are the joint, performatory activities that occur in the ZPD of infancy and early childhood. Unencumbered by knowing what (or even that) language is, ignorant of the societal rules by which one is judged a competent speaker, not yet possessing the culturally produced and commodified need to "express oneself" nor the craving for generality and abstraction, very young children do not say, "I don't know how to talk." (Nor do their caregivers say that to them.) They are marvelous meaning makers—because and as they, jointly with others, perform beyond themselves.

Knowing plays no part in the developmental activity of very early childhood. Babies say things before they know how or what to say. They babble, use words and make meaning as an inseparable part of the process of participating in social life before they know how to participate. In the ZPD/through performance, they "rise above themselves" and are "a head taller" than they are (Vygotsky, 1978, 1987); they engage in the "being ahead of yourself" activity (Newman & Holzman, 1993). As with play, so with games which, in Wittgenstein's sense, are pretty much the full time activity of life for the very young. Children play games without knowing the rules; this is, in fact, how they come to learn the rules. But neither games nor play can, in isolation, account for the existence or development of language (or of anything else). A synthesis of Vygotsky's play and Wittgenstein's games enriches each of them and further involves them in the creating of a new, nonepistemological, therapeutic, and performatory approach to human life.

I am not alone in marveling at how much better learners children are than adults. They learn much more, much better, and much faster. They learn in the Vygotskian sense of learning: "The only 'good learning' is that which is in advance of development" (Vygotsky, 1987, p. 89). It seems that the more we know, the less "good learning" we do. When it comes to language, for example, the better we know the correct way to play language-games (to *use* language), the worse we are at playing them the way young children do (language as *activity*). The first language-game—played over and over and over again in early childhood—is "Making Meaning (Jointly) in the ZPD" (Newman & Holzman, 1996, p. 191). Paradoxically, playing this game in its infinite variations is what makes using language in societally appropriate ways possible at all. And yet, the better we know language societally, the more distant language activity becomes. The rules of language—placed "out there"—come to govern us to the extent that we have forgotten how and/or have few environments that support babbling, playing new language-games, or performing as meaning makers.

Obviously, school-age children and adults are not infants or toddlers. Ten-year-olds who cannot read and 16-year-olds who find school boring are not babbling babies. Yet, it does not follow from their differences that with middle childhood (and adulthood) should come an entirely different approach to learning (and to life). Vygotsky's work makes clear that learning and development in early childhood depend on creating environments that support learning–leading–development, not on identifying problems and trying to solve them (the educational version being to assess what a child does not know "by her or himself," then isolate that skill or subject matter and "teach" it).

The learning–leading–development environments of early childhood are performatory ZPDs. It seems to me that a Vygotskian–Wittgensteinian approach to learning (and life) beyond early childhood must, likewise, be one that creates performatory ZPDs. If we want to help school-age children learn, then we must help them perform.

The elements out of which to shape the ZPD will, of course, be different. For one thing, school-age children already know a lot, including quite a bit about knowing. These children already know that "you're supposed to know things" and "how to do things *by yourself.*" School-age children already know that the time for pretend play is over, if not permanently, then relegated to nonlearning situations (i.e., not in school). They already know the culturally accepted ways to speak and do many everyday things, and they already know that there is something called knowledge (if not yet the word). What these children already know turns out to be an impediment to performing—to doing what they do not know how to do, going beyond themselves, playing without knowing the rules. Thus, performing after early childhood needs to be a volitional, conscious act. Babies perform without knowing they are performing, but once we have performed our way into societally appropriate behavior, we have to *choose* to perform. We have to be directed to perform by others or ourselves.

SOME WAYS TO PERFORM YOUR LIFE

Our developing development community consists of many performance spaces. Societally speaking, the size, shape, and location of the ecologically valid laboratories (the development projects) created by the community have transformed many times over the years. However, these varied therapeutic, cultural, and educational programs share a practice of method—they help people of all ages to perform their lives. Saving the discussion of the

Barbara Taylor School—the elementary education laboratory—for chapter 7, here I describe some of the other programs currently in operation.

Social Therapy Centers. Social therapy is the noninterpretive, non-diagnostic psychotherapeutic approach practiced by Newman and his colleagues in therapy centers in the New York City area, and in Boston, Philadelphia, San Francisco, Atlanta, and Washington, DC. We have been writing on this developmental–clinical approach to emotional development and its roots and major influences since the late 1970s.[3]

As it has evolved over the past 20 years, social therapy is an approach to emotional problems and pain that is unscientific and nonpsychological. In fact, it is more accurate to say that social therapy is an antipsychology in that it views developmental activity as curative—a view that challenges the deep-rooted bias of psychology against development (i.e., the human practice of development, not the psychologists' construct). Most therapeutic approaches take behavioral change, intrapsychic awareness, or problem solving to be the way to help people in emotional pain; the presumption is that, once people are helped in this way, perhaps they can develop further. In contrast, the social therapeutic approach rests on the belief that emotional development is what is necessary to do anything about emotional pain. Social therapists do not engage with clients in "the process of constructing a private, individuated self that must, for better or worse, relate to 'a social world' (psychology's myth of development)"; instead, their work is the "continuous and qualitative transformation of the determining circumstances, creating new emotional meaning, performing new emotional forms of life" (Newman & Holzman, 1996, p. 167).

Creating new emotional forms of life is a relational, performatory, and philosophical activity that takes place among heterogeneous groups of people. (There are no social therapy groups composed of people with similar identifying problems or similar social or cultural identities.) Both time-limited and ongoing groups are offered, as are day-long workshops and "life performance trainings." Social therapy centers continually experiment with innovative formats, such as multifamily groups composed of four to five families (children and parents), and a "community group" in which approximately 50 people serve as the "collective therapist" for a social therapist. What is common to all is the role of the therapist as a director of Wittgensteinian language-games and organizer of Vygotskian ZPDs for the continuous performance of emotional development.

---

[3]For academically oriented discussions, see Holzman (1996), Holzman and Newman (1979), Newman (1991), Newman and Holzman (1993, 1996, 1997), and the series of articles in Holzman and Polk (1988). See also Newman's books for general audiences (1994, 1996).

People "in" social therapy are exposed to the range of activities of the community, including the programs described here (the Manhattan therapy center shares space with the Castillo Theatre). Some people participate in other activities (the most common being attending theatrical performances or taking classes); others simply come to therapy and are not involved in anything else that might be going on. (See Holzman, 1995c, for discussion of the ways social therapy controversially challenges some of psychotherapy's institutional conventions.)

Center for Developmental Learning and the East Side Institute for Short Term Psychotherapy.   The Institute and the Center are "postmodern" continuing education centers in that their focus is the developmental activity of creating a continuing evolving learning community. Since the late 1980s, more than 75 professionals and lay therapists have completed the Institute's 2-year certificate program in social therapeutic training (the Institute is provisionally chartered by the New York State Board of Regents). Training consists of intensive course work, supervisory groups, and co-leading groups. The trainees' task is to create their learning and supervisory groups; through this collective work, they learn the social therapeutic approach—not as fixed content, but as a developmental modality.

Thousands more have attended classes, workshops, lectures, seminars, practica, and intensive weekend institutes in some aspect of the performatory, developmental approach. The faculty include skilled development directors who support the participants to create a developmental learning environment. A variety of people (some with a professional interest in a particular subject, many more without a practical goal) participate in courses such as "The Performance of Philosophy" and "Discovering (Developing) Vygotsky"; dialogues on "The Nature of Suffering" and "Understanding Practice in Practice"; workshops dealing with abuse, short-term performance work, and the postmodern family; and guest lectures from antipsychiatrists, social constructionists, and alternative medicine methodologists from the United States and abroad.

All Stars Talent Show Network.   Founded in 1985 in the Bronx, in one of the poorest and most underserved neighborhoods in New York City, today the All Stars Talent Show Network is recognized as one of the country's largest and most effective anti-violence programs for inner-city youth. In 1996, more than 30,000 young people, ages 4 to 21, participated in producing and performing in more than 65 shows and auditions throughout New York City and in Newark (New Jersey), Philadelphia, Boston, and Miami. The young people who join the All Stars participate by performing—not only music, dance, and skits but also the activities necessary to produce talent shows, including stage managing, audience building, running sound systems, and handling security. Together, and with a small number of trained adults, they take full responsibility for what they produce and how they produce it. In actively building their own cultural organization (rather than simply appearing in talent shows run by others), members of the All Stars create their own emotional, social, and cultural development. Since 1995 they have produced the annual Phat Friends Awards honoring adults in government, education, entertainment, and other fields whose work supports the development of young people. In 1994, I traveled to Moscow with the producer and three young people from the All Stars to present a symposium, "Developing in a Violent World," at the International Conference on L. S. Vygotsky and the Contemporary Human Sciences (Holzman, 1995b).

The environment of the All Stars is a Vygotskian ZPD in which young people are supported to be other than who they are in a culture in which they are typically overidentified with destructive behavior. More often than not, they are defined by others at a very young age, they adopt the appropriate identity, and they act out the expected roles. Typically this definition and identity include that they have nothing to give. Participating in the All Stars Talent Show Network requires that they perform as builders and givers. In doing so, they discover that they can do so. They become who they are by being who they are not. In this process, they create new options for who and how they want to be—given the often terrible objective conditions of their lives.

These conditions include abusive behavior as the all too often rule and role, with violence having become a rigid form of life—in part because there is little consciousness that it is a form of life. Time and again, we see confrontations between, for example, two angry young men in which it is clear that neither has any idea that they do not *have* to hurt each other, that they can change the form of life; they can be who they are not, they can perform.

The approach to violence this program takes is perhaps unique in that it is not directed to educating young people about the impact of violence. The reason for this is that we do not believe that violence can be stopped. Ours is a methodological position (although it is surely given added legitimacy by empirics—violence among young people continues to rise and to be their main killer). Contemporary violence is a by-product of the lack of development in our culture and, in my opinion, can no more be stopped than can educational failure. What is possible, however, is for development to begin again. The All Star's approach to violence is to ignore it—and create development. In this way it practically–critically instantiates Wittgenstein's antipsychological, antiepistemological, antiphilosophical philosophy. In as close to a maxim as he ever comes,

Wittgenstein said, "What is your disease? You ask this question again and again—How can one make you stop doing this? By drawing your attention to something else" (Wittgenstein, 1980, p. 60).

Pregnant Productions.   Modeled on the All Stars, Pregnant Productions is an after-school, teen pregnancy prevention program open to both girls and boys (operating in some of New York City's poorest communities) that ignores the "problem" of teen pregnancy and focuses on development instead. With the support of adults trained in the performatory–developmental approach, the young people produce cultural events that address the complex social, economic, and emotional issues of sex, sexuality, growing up, and pregnancy. In creating their own production company and performances, these teens and preteens learn that they can make all kinds of choices and take responsibility for them. These may or may not include whether and when to become pregnant.

Performance of a Young Lifetime.   This after-school program in a South Bronx elementary school was piloted in the spring of 1996. Under siege from the New York City Board of Education because of poor student attendance and academic performance, the school received funds to provide counseling services for a portion of the children. Performance of a Young Lifetime was created as a way to help these children create something positive in and out of their lives. Counselors trained in the performatory–developmental approach led groups of children in Grades 1 to 6 in improvisation games, creating skits that were scenes from their lives, and putting these diverse elements together in a public performance at the end of the school year.

As with the All Stars and Pregnant Productions, the youngsters had the opportunity to make all kinds of decisions—what the play should be, if they wanted to perform at any particular moment, if and how to take direction, what to do if someone made fun of them or was disruptive—and to take responsibility for themselves and for the performance. They were able to see themselves and one another apart from such already well-practiced school roles as troublemaker, nerd, and dummy through performing these and other, new roles—inseparable from creating the environment in which they could perform.

These are some of the projects (performance stages) of the developing development community.[4]

---

[4]Other projects include the Castillo Theatre, a 14-year-old off-off Broadway theater, and Performance of a Lifetime, interactive growth theater for nonprofessionals.

Part III

Radical Educational Alternatives and Their Developmental Potential

♦ ♦ ♦

From the beginning of the American public school system there have always been educators, parents, and students who have declined to participate and instead created alternative schools and alternatives to schools, such as homeschooling. (The oldest alternative school still in existence dates back to 1786, according to Mintz, 1995, p. 10.) In this century, the late 1960s and early 1970s saw the founding of many alternatives, followed by a tapering off for several years. In the last 15 years, there has been a dramatic increase, with more than 60% of existing educational alternatives—estimated at more than 6,000—having been founded since the early 1980s (Mintz, 1995, p. 10). Although there are varied and complex political, cultural, and religious motivations for alternative schooling, the desire for a greater level of autonomy and participation in creating more educational choices seems clear. For this reason alone, the structure, organization, and philosophy of alternatives seems worthy of serious examination by educators, educational researchers, and policymakers.

Another reason to study the alternative schools movement and alternative schools is that they are remarkably successful by traditional standards. The research that has been done (and there is not very much of it) consistently shows the superiority of alternative schools—both public and independent—on a wide variety of measures (see, e.g., Miller, 1992; Mintz, 1995; Wood, 1992, for discussions of studies and specific schools). It is the public alternatives such as magnet and charter schools that we tend to hear about; rarely do independent alternatives receive either media coverage or research consideration. This is unfortunate because it is the independent school that is more likely to attempt to create and implement a qualitatively different methodology from traditional models. We can learn (discover, be provoked, see in new ways) from what their independence allows them to do, perhaps in a way that frees us to "now go on."

It is in this spirit of developmental learning that three independent educational alternatives are presented in the following chapters. They are, in sometimes overlapping and sometimes contrasting ways, radical alternatives to current educational models in being practical challenges not only to the organization of schooling but to its philosophical structure. As the story of each school unfolds, its integrity is hopefully preserved even as my activity–theoretic, nonepistemological, and therapeutic perspective is the lens through which it is being seen. For, as should be clear by now, I am seeking to discover what is developmental—in the revolutionary Vygotskian sense of developmental activity—about these radical alternatives. This entails examining to what extent they are (or can be understood as) nonepistemological, activity-based, and performatory.

Chapter 5

Project Golden Key:
A Russian Experiment
in Developmental Education

◆ ◆ ◆

The 10 of us piled into a small bus bound for a developmental education center on the outer edges of the Moscow region about an hour's drive from the center of the city. We ranged in age from 12-year-old Lance Bennett, an African-American eighth grader from Queens, New York and Jessica Betancourt, a Puerto Rican junior high school student from the South Bronx, New York to 70-year-old Gita Vygodskaya, Moscow resident and daughter of the renowned Lev Vygotsky. Also among us were Vygodskaya's daughter Elena Kravtsova and her husband Gennady Kravtsov, the originators of the educational approach implemented at the center and numerous others in cities throughout the former Soviet Union; four psychologists from the Institute of Psychology at the University of Belgrade; and Pam Lewis and Danny Forbes, the producer and assistant producer of the All Stars Talent Show Network to which Lance and Jessica belonged. All of us were participants in an international conference on the relevance of Vygotsky's work to the human sciences, sponsored by the Russian Academies of Education and of Sciences. Pam, Danny, Jessica, and Lance were co-presenters with me in a session entitled, "The Vygotskian Talent Show: Developing in a Violent World." Our trip was made possible by contributions from many individual supporters of the developing development community of which the All Stars is a showcase project.

As we drove, the conversations ebbed and flowed, as what were essentially three groups of people who knew each other well and were strangers to the others (and the others' languages and cultures) crossed, retreated, and then crossed again the boundaries between us. Those who had attended the All Stars session the day before spoke eagerly and easily with the young people. Elena Kravtsova gave us some background on the center we would be visiting and the general philosophy of the approach she and her husband—both psychologists—had developed. She spoke about the dire need to transform Russian education in the face of the growing alienation of Russian youth and the importance of play, performance, and role-playing experiences.

When we arrived we were greeted in the muddy graveled yard by a delegation of children and adults bearing flowers and bread (a Russian show of hospitality). We were ushered into a room that contained a large replica of the world's climactic and geological zones, complete with models of plants and animals. A long table had been set up at one end with samovars of hot tea and plates of little sandwiches and sweets. As we ate and drank, the young people got together, conversing in their own languages as they showed each other many things, from the Russian's miniature monkeys and lizards in the replica of the world's temperature zones to the American's Walkman and video camera. Several of the Russian children who spoke some English asked Jessica, Lance, and Danny to become their pen pals.

We then were ushered upstairs for an elaborate staged performance by the students that included singing, dancing, some stand-up comedy, and several dramatic scenes. When the director was told that the American young people were producers of talent shows, she invited them to create a show right then. Danny emceed and Jessica stage managed the show (as they often did in New York). The portable stereo was set up, and Danny introduced Lance who rapped—first alone and then with Danny. Then everyone—adults and children—danced to American rap and to rhythm and blues.

After an hour-long discussion with the staff in which their pride in their work and love for their students was evident, we were all given small gifts (a Russian tradition) and said our goodbyes.

Visiting a school modeled on work of Vygotsky's granddaughter and being accompanied on the one hand by his daughter and on the other hand by youth leaders from New York's inner city was a very moving experience. The meeting seemed historic: here were builders of (participants in) two very different Vygotskian development projects—the All Stars, a uniquely American cultural phenomenon, and a nongraded elementary school in a suburb of Moscow—brought together by Gita Vygodskaya, one of the people who had made it possible for Vygotsky's work to be carried on and, hopefully, advanced. *That* we were meeting was far more meaningful than what, if anything, any of us learned from the encounter.

EDUCATION FOR A NEW GENERATION

The transition to a pedagogy whose aim is the holistic development of the child is a task which requires the restructuring of the whole life of adults and children. To use the terminology of Lev Vygotsky, what is required is that the entire "situation of development" be changed. The principles of Vygotsky's cultural–historical theory of development—in particular, the principle of the unity of affect and intellect—provides the theoretical framework for the project, *Golden Key*. (Kravtsova & Kravtsov, 1996)[1]

It is important to remember that Vygotsky's work was not at all well known in his home country; consequently, the educational system in Russia and the other independent states of the former Soviet Union was virtually unaffected by his views of learning/instruction and development. Soviet education changed little over the decades; as a bureaucratic and conservative institution, it was resistant to organic change in either curriculum or process. In this it was more extreme, but not qualitatively different, from our educational system. By most accounts, Soviet education accomplished what are perhaps modest, but not insignificant, goals: The production of young adults who were literate, knowledgeable about Russian and European history and culture (especially literature and poetry), and trained in the basics of mathematics and the physical sciences. In addition, as most adults who spent any time in the former Soviet Union can tell you, the experience of talking with young people was particularly fascinating because of the kinds of things they knew about (American writers and presidents) and did not know about (social conditions, music, sports, and film). All that is changed now—except for the schools.

Elena Kravtsova and Gennady Kravtsov (the Russian linguistic convention requires the feminine ending on a woman's name) are among many educators, social scientists, and parents in Russia who began work to transform education and schooling even before the breakup of the Soviet Union. In addition to hundreds of independent schools springing up all over the country, there are some major centralized and/or university-connected efforts at wide-scale reforms; textbooks are being rewritten, teachers are receiving training in new teaching methods, and developmental and educational research from the West is being disseminated.

The Golden Key project was founded in this climate. Its name derives from the key that Pinnochio seeks in the Russian version of the classic fairy tale. In this *Pinnochio*, written by Tolstoy and known to every Russian child, the wooden puppet finds a golden key that opens a special door, after which people transform—becoming inclusive, happy, respectful, loving, and giving to each other. This is the goal of the Golden Key developmental education project—to create an environment where children's learning is not separate from their emotional growth nor from their creating happy, joyful lives. Its

---

[1]The description and analysis in this chapter come from three main sources: personal observations; a combination of official documents outlining the Golden Key project and personal written communication from Kravtsova and Kravtsov; and conversations with them and Elena Lampert Schepel, a Russian Vygotskian scholar and educational practitioner now living in the United States.

authors, concerned with the ways in which education has contributed to the crisis in post-Soviet Russian society—particularly to the "poor health of the new generation"—place an emphasis on the affective dimension of life because this is one of the things that is needed to break down the profound alienation produced by and in traditional schools. To do so is a major task necessitating that "the principles and organization of pedagogical process must be changed" (Kravtsova & Kravtsov, personal communication, December 1996).

The Golden Key project began with the establishment of one child center in Moscow in 1989. During Perestroika, the Russian Ministry of Education started accepting proposals for alternatives to the official state curriculum; Golden Key became one of them. Currently, the model is implemented in 30 child centers in cities of Russia and other now independent republics, with 5 more planned. (This represents a tiny percentage of educational institutions for young children.) The foundations for the approach with older children has been written, with expansion into junior high school currently planned.[2]

The changes effected in this experimental project are guided by Vygotsky's understanding of learning and development as fundamentally social, relational activity, his discovery of the ZPD as where/how learning–leading–development occurs, and the developmental nature of play. Further, the shaping of the educational environment builds on certain characteristics of the home and family environment that are seen as supportive of the development of preschool children.

This new model for elementary education challenges the way teachers, children, and their parents currently organize their relationships. For example, as in the United States, it is typical in Russia for home and school to be separate spheres of life and distant from each other. To the originators of Golden Key, it is not enough that parents know what goes on at school and teachers what goes on at home; parents and other family members are involved in the life of the school, building it as a community, and sharing the burdens.

The traditional breakdown of education into preschool, kindergarten, and elementary school is also reorganized. Taking this distinction to be "artificial" and developmentally detrimental, Golden Key has neither preschool nor kindergarten, but serves children from ages 3 to 10. These children are understood to belong to the same cultural–historical "epoch" of development (infancy and adolescence are two other "epochs") and are related to as an evolving and ever-changing group.

---

[2]In a recent conversation, Elena Kravtsova informed me of the establishment of the Institute of Psychology After Vygotsky at the new Russian State Humanistic University in Moscow where research and study of this Vygotskian approach will be undertaken.

THE DIALECTIC OF CREATING A ZPD

The key characteristics of the developmental education model of Golden Key are the following:

1. The role and position of the teacher is transformed from educating children to *sharing life with children*. Within this shared life activity, the teacher can "solve pedagogical problems." (Teachers undergo intensive in-service training.)
2. To overcome the existing alienation of family from school, the life of children in school is opened to the parents. Furthermore, it is believed that "the system of relationships in the school should complete the relationships in the family."
3. To maximize positive, growthful communication and social relationships (which are thought to be the major conditions for the development of consciousness and personality), children are placed into *multiage groups*. It is in such heterogeneous groupings that play develops spontaneously and other forms of developmental activity emerge. The practice of separating children by age, in contrast, stifles this kind of learning–leading–development.
4. The usual school practices that make a separation between intellect and affect are transformed through the other three characteristics. Learning (what they call "solving pedagogical tasks") is subordinate to the values of a happy life and maximum positive development, and occurs in the context of the overall life activities of the children and adults.

Between 60 and 150 children from the ages of 3 to 10 attend each center. They are organized into multiage groups of 15 to 25 children (with each age equally represented) and two specially trained adults. Parent and guest visits are common, as is interaction between groups.

There are several ways to describe the organization of the centers. First, their design is based on features of a "good family"—one in which all the adults participate in children's upbringing and children have equal rights with adults. It is this system of relationships that, it is believed, is maximally developmental for children. The teachers' task is to create—in this sense—a large family of children and adults (other teachers and family members) that completes and broadens a child's "natural" family. Many daily activities are preplanned by the adults; nevertheless, the children are supported to organize and plan their activities. In addition to daily meetings, discussions about plans and the organization of learning activities are encouraged. Conversation plays a major role in the life of the school.

A second way the centers are organized is around life events that "the group lives through together" and for which leading learning activities are created. *Event* does not mean what it does in English; what is actually being referred to here is a form of development.[3] The Russian word *cobu-tije*—roughly translated as "event" when it is pronounced as one word and as "co-existence" when pronounced as two—has special meaning in Russian philosophy that is difficult to convey in English. The term refers simultaneously to interrelated concepts: Things that are different from routine life (event)—in this sense, event is drama—and the mutual reality of adults and children (co-existence). The system of events, or drama, is considered one of the most important tools of emotional development. The primacy of drama in this educational approach is truly innovative within Russian schools, where it has never been part of any curriculum (except for the role-playing common in kindergarten).

One of the prominent life events that organizes group activities is the change of seasons. The coming of spring, for example, influences the life of the group through the themes of the games the children play and the "real" activities they participate in such as building birdhouses and gardening. "These events, making the life of the children meaningful, are always somehow different every year. Besides the events, which become traditional, new games, books and topics for conversations emerge. Children visit new places, participate in socially meaningful activities (such as preparing presents and visiting people)" (Kravtsova & Kravtsov, personal communication, December 1996). Within the seasons, each month frames activities and topics subordinate to those of the season, similarly for each week within a month.

These activities are, no doubt, similar in some ways to the common practices in traditional schools that utilize seasonal and other changes to teach elements of the curriculum. However, the overall educational philosophy and Kravtsova and Kravtsov's way of speaking suggest that they are not viewed as merely contextual nor that it is their instrumentality that is primary. The focus in their language is on the logic and meaning of temporal and seasonal elements: for example, "a week has its own logic, its own topic (subordinate to those of the month and season) and its culmination ... every day in the week has its own meaning, its place in the development of a topic" (Kravtsova & Kravtsov, personal communication, December 1996). It is time, change, history, and the like as elements of human life—as activity—that makes them important elements in this form of developmental education.

A third level of organization is the structuring of learning activities and specific learning materials that consciously makes use of the age dynamics within the groups. The nature of the multiage groups "as a complete organism changes all the time; its sensitivity and ability to work as a group with a learning material, to discuss and make sense of problems is constantly developing, becoming more sophisticated and varied" (Kravtsova & Kravt-

---

[3]I was aided in this attempt to convey the meaning and importance of "event" by Elena Lampert Schepel.

sov, personal communication, December 1996). This recognition that it is the group that develops is critically important in creating ZPDs. At the same time as the abilities of the older children in the group define the level of difficulty of a particular activity, the younger children can and do engage with the materials in varying ways and at different levels. The "older" the group (the totality) the greater are the learning possibilities *for every child within the group*. What is being described here, it seems to me, is the creative and emergent quality of the ZPD—in which the constant dialectical inter-play between *the total environment* and elements within it creates/is developmental activity.

Kravtsova and Kravtsov provided details of Golden Key for the first 4 years of the program. Their descriptions (consistent with my observations) are further revealing of the different conception of education, learning, development, play, and the relationship between individual and group that underlie this experimental Vygotskian project.

For children between ages 3 and 6, the educational content (activities and materials) is geared to four emergent abilities: (a) the ability to organize the environment based on the goals of a particular activity; (b) orientation in time and the ability to plan; (c) the ability to use specific qualities of various materials in the children's own activities; and (d) the ability to analyze their own activity and reflect upon themselves as agents. Although these are inseparably connected and always at play, each year of the 4-year program being a different one "leads" the others in guiding activities. For example, in the first year the major task is orienting to the environment (the school, the community) and organizing their own learning environment *as a group*. Kravtsova and Kravtsov (personal communication, December 1996) described some of what occurs:

> This task is solved with the help of specially designed learning materials. Children design various plans and schemes that are organic in their everyday activities. For example, children take a trip to the park and when they return create a plan of their route, marking houses, fences, trees, big puddles, etc. This plan lives in the group for a couple of weeks, becoming more and more detailed. There are also other plans and schemas of a smaller scale. Children invite guests from other groups to their group, enclosing a plan to find the way to their room with the invitation. During theater performances children create flyers, programs and tickets—this is also the creation of a particular environment-space. And the exhibiting of their paintings is connected with mastery of exposition space.

In the second year, the study of history and time are of key importance. Children travel in a time machine and learn Russian history. They create plays and play at producing films, performing (and thereby becoming familiar with) the work of producers, scriptwriters, actors, and designers. The third year continues and deepens activities geared to understanding historical epochs and introduces the employment of crafts and folk art. In the fourth year, the learning of the first three years is reshaped toward the children becoming more conscious of themselves as "active agents of their activity in the overall flow of life." It is important to emphasize that it is not the child's year (first, second, and so on) being referred to, but the multiage group's year, lest the above be understood as equivalent to or even similar to grade level. The organizing principle (the philosophical structure) of this alternative educational model is the ongoing development of the group *as it creates itself as a group* that is developing and changing. To me, this focus on the group is what—in Vygotskian fashion—allows for the "good learning" that Golden Key documents for all its children.

THE LEARNING SUBJECT
AND THE SUBJECT OF LEARNING

Within the three levels of organization just described, the children and adults at child centers implementing the Golden Key model interact in a variety of ways. There is the "family group," small group study and play, and individual child–adult work (the latter is referred to as a businesslike partnership). These different kinds of interactions are understood to be important for development but for different reasons. Unlike traditional schools, in which group work is often viewed as a pragmatic necessity, the implementers of Golden Key believe that children—even those who are slow at grasping material—learn optimally by participating in "collectively distributed activity."

The purpose of individual work with students is not to help them better learn material presented in a lesson; it is not supplemental (to make up for some lack of knowledge transfer due to the nature of group activities) nor is it remedial. Rather, it serves a different purpose from group lessons and collective activity. The individual child–adult partnership functions to give every child everyday experience and practice in *building a learning relationship* with an adult. This relationship ("individual partnership") goes through qualitative changes in the course of its history, and its role in the learning process also changes.

The concept of *learning activity* is important to Golden Key's philosophy and pedagogy, particularly in relation to the forming of the individual partnership. Within activity theory generally, and in the dominant contemporary Russian reading of Vygotsky, learning activity is a specific (usually understood to be age-related) form of activity that is essential for children to eventually become able to learn and study independently. The success or failure of developing this ability depends, according to this view, on the type and quality of adult–child interactions.

It is not clear to what extent Golden Key adheres to the strict Russian concept of learning activity (as put forth and developed into school practice by Davydov and Elkonin) that restricts the ZPD to an adult–child dyadic unit which somehow, through its interaction around a certain learning material, creates a kind of transference of knowledge or skill. It is stated that children who attend centers in which the Golden Key project is implemented acquire "developed learning activity" by the end of the program. This means, among other things, that they "can reflect, regulate and control their activity," and that they "have a high degree of independent creative work, including mastering general principles and methods of solving learning tasks" (Kravtsova & Kravtsov, personal communication, December 1996).

On the one hand, the emphasis on creating the group as a developmental learning environment and the focus on the ZPD-building potential of multiage groups certainly suggest that Golden Key's originators have a more activistic and dialectical conception of learning activity. Their philosophy and practice strongly suggest that, for them, it is human beings that are the subjects of learning. On the other hand, in discussing the special role of individual teaching, the activity of building the relationship (the developmental learning environment), while stated, is not emphasized in the same way as it is in discussions of the group.

Golden Key does not function with a subject-based curriculum. Learning is unequivocally activity-based. Although I am not suggesting that by "activity" they intend, as I do, *revolutionary activity*, there is the recognition that learning–leading–development is the simultaneous building of a developmental learning environment and the developmental learning it supports. There is at least a critical eye toward the knowing paradigm and the equating of learning with knowing. Moreover, the dominant role of dramatization and play and the organization of school life around "events" (drama) are consistent with the kind of revolutionary reading of Vygotsky described in chapters 3 and 4. The Golden Key project seems to be all about children performing beyond themselves.

At the same time, there are clearly delineated subjects, not in the usual sense of subject (such as math or reading), but *things* to be learned nevertheless. For example, among the many expected learning outcomes are the following: "solve tasks using arithmetic operations," "find their way in an unknown city," "know existing flora and fauna," and "define North, South, East and West" (Kravtsova & Kravtsov, personal communication, December 1996). There is, thereby, the presumption (and promotion) of an existing body of knowledge as a desired product of learning activities.

Kravtsova and Kravtsov stated that one cause of problems in Russian schools is that "students do not have the opportunity to become the subject of their learning but must always carry out somebody else's assignment and do what adults tell them to" (Kravtsova & Kravtsov, personal communication, December 1996). The delineation of specific learning outcomes for their students (decided in advance) seems to go against Golden Key's principle of full participation and further, the tool-and-resultish character of much of how the centers are organized. What is at issue here is not whether learning outcomes are desirable or not, but rather how far in deconstructing traditional schooling this unique alternative has gone. In organizing an educational environment according to the principle that "children's learning happens in the course of their everyday life and in the traditional types of children's activity (play)" (Kravtsova & Kravtsov, personal communication, December 1996), Golden Key's originators have broken down some of the socially constructed boundaries that are integral to the knowing paradigm—the boundaries that form subjects and disciplines; the boundary between learning and playing; the boundaries between family, school, and community; and the boundary between subjective and objective knowledge.

Without question, this approach is a radical departure from an educational system in which, only a few years ago, millions of children and teachers across the vast expanse of the Soviet Union opened the same books at the same moment of the day and did the same lesson in rote learning. The knowing paradigm was as deeply, if somewhat differently, entrenched in Soviet education as it has been in American and other Western systems of education. However, the political and economic changes that have accompanied its collapse and the formation of newly independent nations have brought sociocultural changes that provide a different environment in which efforts to transform and democratize schools is occurring.

One important change is the swing from collectivism to individualism. Entrenched in a modern world view—in which understanding is dualistic, possibilities are dichotomies, and change is merely opposition to what is—to a large extent Russia (and other formerly communist countries) are effecting the abandonment of enforced collectivism (a positive move) by way of unself-consciously and uncritically embracing extreme individualism. This is merely the flip side of a dualistic coin. Ironically (and unfortunately), many Russian psychologists now eagerly look to American psychology for guidance in understanding human life in terms of the very "self-contained and isolated individual" and "knowing mind" that so many American, European, and growing numbers of so-called Third World psychologists so vigorously critique. Taking such a route is understandably tempting. That the Golden Key project has gone as far as it has in resisting it and, instead, is attempting to forge a new practice of human learning and development that breaks with the individual–collective dichotomy is all the more impressive in light of the intense pressures in their society in general and the specific pressure within the fields of psychology and pedagogy to Westernize (de-revolutionize, de-dialecticize) Vygotsky. They appear to have heeded Vygotsky's maxim that "the only good learning is that which is in advance of development" (Vygotsky, 1978, p. 89) through reshaping elements of Russian and post-Soviet culture into environments in which children can perform ahead of themselves.

Chapter 6

When Democratic Education Is Developmental: The Sudbury Valley School Model

◆ ◆ ◆

The Sudbury Valley School, in Framingham, Massachusetts (a suburb 20 miles west of Boston) opened in 1968, a date that both suggests its mission and philosophy and belies its continued existence after nearly 30 years. The activism of the 1960s was marked by thousands of alternative institutions; parents and teachers who set up free, alternative, and community schools in their own image of what learning and education should be were among those who ventured out on their own. Few such projects lasted more than a decade. Most folded after a few years, whereas others abandoned their radicalness either through becoming incorporated into the bureaucracy of the school system or becoming institutionalized themselves.

Sudbury Valley School, which has maintained a radical educational philosophy over 30 years, is an exception. During this time it has grown quantitatively (from 60 to 200 students) but also qualitatively—more than 15 schools across the United States have modeled themselves on Sudbury Valley. It is also unique among alternative schools in having its own small press and publishing books and essays on its philosophy and the role of schools in the contemporary world, tapes, a monthly newsletter, and a variety of documents about its current students' activities and updates on former students. Since 1991, dozens of Sudbury Valley School "starter kits" have been purchased each year by people interested in founding their own alternative schools.

Sudbury Valley School—the place—immediately struck me as "a haven in a heartless world" (Lasch, 1976). Located in a century-old former mansion on 10 acres adjacent to a state forest to which the school has access, it is simply beautiful. It is also peaceful, not in the sense of being quiet and orderly, but more the way we envision an old-time family picnic might have been—bustling and harmonious, with many different sized groups of people of different ages doing many different things—playing ball, climbing trees, cooking, eating, listening to music, talking, flirting, reading, taking photographs, writing poetry, dancing, playing cards, and sleeping.

Two hundred students, ages 4 to 19, and 14 adults (a combination of full- and part-time staff) spend their days inside the building and on the grounds involved in a great variety of activities that they themselves generate. Along with parents or guardians, they operate the school in a democratic fashion modeled on the New England town meeting. Aside from rules and regulations concerning safety, attendance, use of equipment, and respect for each other, activities are voluntary and spontaneous. There are no grades, no curriculum, and no classes or teachers (unless one or more students decide they want to learn a particular thing and ask a staff member to teach it). Daniel Greenberg (1987), a former Columbia University physics professor who was one of its founders and is its chief "philosophical writer," described Sudbury Valley as a "perpetual recess" (p. 24).

The student body is local. The majority of students are White and come from middle-class and lower middle-class families in which both parents work. Many students begin part-time jobs as teenagers to help pay their tuition. In earlier years, Sudbury Valley attracted many "bummed out" adolescents, most of whom attended for only 1 year. The average age was 16 and the turnover was extremely high. Since the late 1980s, the school has attracted more and more younger students who stay longer. In 1996, the average age was 13, the average stay 3 years.

The foundation of Sudbury Valley School practice is the belief that the individual liberties set forth by the founders of the nation "will never really be secure until our youth, throughout the crucial formative years of their minds and spirits, are nurtured in a school environment that embodies these basic American truths" (Greenberg, 1987, p. 14). The school's founders, therefore, set out to create an environment that was democratic rather than autocratic, governed by clear rights and due process, and one that guarded the individual rights of students. They believed that in such an environment intellectual creativity, professional excellence, personal responsibility, social tolerance, and political liberty would flourish (Greenberg, 1987).

In carrying out what is, essentially, a libertarian philosophy, Sudbury Valley is consistent and nonhypocritical. It has created structures and processes that are attempts to promote individual choice exercised in the context of a greater community. At the level of the management and running of the school—for example, who will be hired as staff, how monies will be spent, who will receive a high school diploma (students must demonstrate that they are responsible members of the community at large)—democratic process dominates, with these kinds of decisions being reached through debate and voting. The administrative body of the school is the weekly School Meeting. Composed of all students and staff, this body carries out day to day operations and the policies of the Assembly (the governing body of the school). In this way, members of the school community have the opportunity to effect change in the school.

At the level of daily activities and interactions, each student decides for her or himself how to spend each day. The adults are there to help them—if asked—create their own learning environments. The most recent report from the New England Association of Schools and Colleges (an accreditation body) reflects on "the flexibility the school shows in meeting student requests ... the school does not minimize the work necessary to gain knowledge but strives to create an environment where students can find whatever help they need" (Sudbury Valley Press, 1996, pp. 20–21). Long-term student interests are brought to the School Meeting for consideration. A "Corporation" might be formed and funds allocated for the learning project; when interest in it wanes, the Corporation is disbanded (again, by the School Meeting).

Sudbury Valley School makes no concessions to the institutionalized need for standardized measures of evaluation. In spite of the fact that the school provides no documentation, graduates gain admission to and matriculate in a wide variety of colleges and universities. Greenberg and Sadofsky (1992) suggested that the process by which Sudbury Valley School graduates make decisions about pursuing postsecondary school education and applying to schools and, once accepted, how they function as students is more deliberative, informed, and mature than the route taken by the typical high school senior. The remarks of a 27-year-old woman, a former student who is now a social worker, added strength to this generalization:

> Kids from Sudbury are used to talking. They talk a lot. Coming from that school and having to explain it, gives you sort of a leg up. You present as responsible, as articulate, as thinking. You're used to talking to adults.... You're used to intensity in classes. You're used to designing your own schedule. You're used to setting aside time to study because no one's going to do it for you ... what's a little bit hard at first is tests. It takes about one semester and that's it. You're fine. (Greenberg & Sadofsky, 1992, p. 48)

LEARNING AT SUDBURY VALLEY

The Sudbury Valley School founders and staff have written extensively and critically about learning theories that underlie traditional educational practices, but they make no pretense of having developed a theory themselves. In fact, the subtext of their discussions is that there is no need for such a theory. The attempt to comprehend the process of learning through theory construction, according to Greenberg, has created more problems than it has solved (Greenberg, 1987). He noted:

> In order to make up for the feeling of inadequacy in confronting a process that we don't really comprehend, we … label something "learning" and measure it. Then we're comfortable, because at least then we have the feeling that we have a grasp on the problem. We don't really follow the process, but in lieu of a profound understanding of what's going on, we find something and say, "Let's declare that to be learning, by consensus" … This is basically what the entire educational system the world over has done: quantify learning by breaking it up into measurable pieces—curricula, courses, hours, tests, and grades … What does it mean to learn [for example] American history? (pp. 24–25)

The learning that goes on at Sudbury Valley (and Greenberg is certain that learning—lots of it—does go on there) does not fit the accepted (knowledge-based) conception of learning. Greenberg (1987) identified four assumptions of the accepted view of learning: that (some) one knows *what* ought to be learned by people, *when* it ought to be learned, *how* it ought to be learned, and *by whom* each thing ought to be learned (p. 42). Together, these assumptions are the lenses through which people have been socialized in our culture to judge whether learning is occurring or not. The dilemma for Sudbury Valley and other schools that do not adhere to this model of learning—for people constantly ask if their students are learning anything—is that without these assumptions (i.e., when they are violated) the viewer becomes, as it were, "blind."

The belief in individual liberties that, as I noted, forms the basis of the Sudbury Valley School model shapes what Greenberg (1987) saw to be problematic in these assumptions about learning, as seen in the following comments:

> That one knows how to identify *by whom* any given subject ought to be learned … is the most insidious of all assumptions, but it follows directly from all the other points I have made. Our schools have a sophisticated and ever-improving system for tracking people, and for finding out at an ever earlier age what specific "aptitudes" a person has, so that a precise, narrow track can be determined for this person to follow throughout life. In this society, such a process is exceptionally subtle, because it involves an authoritarian approach within a free culture. By employing a variety of ruses the system produces a process which allows it to inhibit personal freedom without really feeling that this is what is going on. The person doesn't feel that something arbitrary is being done to him—which is in fact what is happening (p. 55)

Greenberg (1987) had little respect for the psychology that buttresses these assumptions: "The assumption is that psychologically one knows enough about the mind to identify aptitudes; and a further assumption is that once one knows aptitudes, one also knows how to track a person so he will in fact reach the goal that is being set out for him. The whole approach is the ultimate in pedagogical and psychological technology. The only trouble is that it is humanly absurd" (pp. 55–56). It is the audacity of psychology's insistence that it can *know* things about the individual mind that mostly offended Greenberg, but not the very conceptions, *individual* and *individual mind*.

Greenberg (1987) identified four general categories of learning that occur at Sudbury Valley. First, there is the development of certain personal character traits, such as independence, self-reliance, open-mindedness, concentration, and resilience in the face of adversity. Second is the learning of social etiquette which includes ease, openness, trust, and articulateness. Sudbury Valley students also learn methodology and creative problem solving—from how to get a piece of equipment to how to study a given subject—including the use of human and archival resources, and are engaged in substantive learning in academic subjects.

When judged either by its own idiosyncratic (which are, generally, more postmodern than modern) standards or traditional ones, Sudbury Valley appears to be successful. Those students who have experienced it "go out into the real world. They make it. They do well. They're well-adjusted and they're not behind" (Greenberg, 1987, p. 24). Over the years, several follow-up studies of former students have been carried out that corroborate this claim, and we turn to the quantitative and qualitative data from the most recent study later in this chapter.

KNOWING AT SUDBURY VALLEY

How complete has the break with modern epistemology been at Sudbury Valley School? Has eliminating classes, grades, subjects, and curriculum—the most obvious institutionally sanctioned carriers of the knowing paradigm—transformed the purpose of schooling away from becoming a knower? How do the staff and students understand the school's effectiveness? Do they view the democratic structure as the key element and, if so, what is their understanding of democracy? To what extent are the school's philosophy and practice coherent? Are either or both consistent with relational, activity–theoretic, developmental learning? To explore these questions, we will need to look in a bit more detail at three characteristics of the Sudbury Valley School model: its rejection of knowledge acquisition; the importance of play; and age-mixing.

Even from the brief description I have presented thus far, a picture begins to emerge of a learning environment that pays remarkably little attention to the acquisition of knowledge. One reason Sudbury Valley School does not have courses or follow a curriculum is because it does not equate education with learning about particular things but rather with personal growth. Comparing its stated aims with traditional ones, for example, those adopted by the National Education Goals Panel ("Goals 2000"), we can see this clearly:

Sudbury Valley—to produce adults who are filled with curiosity, eager to learn all their lives, confident that they can achieve their life goals, and able to enjoy working hard at getting what they really want. (Greenberg, 1992, p. 59)

National Education Goals #3—By the year 2000, all students will leave Grades 4, 8, and 12 having demonstrated competency over challenging subject matter including English, mathematics, science, foreign languages, civics and government, economics, arts, history, and geography, and every school in America will ensure that all students learn to use their minds well, so that they may be prepared for responsible citizenship, further learning, and productive employment in our Nation's modern economy. (National Education Goals Panel, 1996, p. 2)

Courses and subjects are seen as impediments to Sudbury Valley's educational goals. It is believed that the very nature of a course (organized as product) interferes with and disrupts how learning (the process) happens. Sequencing specified content in an orderly path has the effect of ignoring important subjective factors such as what motivates people to pursue learning. Both the kind of "curious probing" with which people often approach a topic initially and the immediacy and intensity that accompany "learning for mastery" are repressed by coursework (Greenberg, 1987).

Greenberg is pointing to the traditional separation of cognition and affect that still dominates psychology and that is pervasive in educational practice. Agreeing with Greenberg, I think that the psychological damage is greater than he has stated. Within the learning-centered environment that is traditional schooling, courses are far too often impediments not only to the person/process-oriented goals of Sudbury Valley but also to the knowledge/product-oriented goals of the National Education Goals Panel. Greenberg did not address the relationship between these two sets of goals, but simply rejected the second set; he does not explore the relationship between learning and development.

In exploring why this might be the case, we will see how the Sudbury Valley School model, although rejecting many elements of the modern epistemological paradigm, still adheres to some of its core conceptions. Ultimately, it does not reject knowing, but substitutes one kind of knowing (about oneself) for another (about things). In philosophy (if not, perhaps, in practice), the school has an individualistic (as opposed to relational) and mentalistic (as opposed to activistic) understanding of human life.

Sudbury Valley's radical (reformist, rather than revolutionary) commitment to freedom of choice and noncoercion is an expression of the school's challenge to prevailing views of what is worth knowing and when it should be known. The Sudbury Valley staff, as far as I can tell, do not hedge on this. Although students eventually all learn to read, for example, the fact that some do not until they are 9, 10, or even older is not a cause for concern. It is not uncommon for new students, particularly adolescents coming from traditional schools, to spend their first year at

Sudbury Valley "doing nothing." Students are free to pursue any subject in whatever manner for as long as they choose.

Sudbury Valley's position on substantive knowledge is fueled as well by its social–cultural analysis, in which the historical transformation from an industrial to a postindustrial society plays the central role. According to this analysis, given this societal transformation, the goals and organization of schooling must, likewise, transform. Yet they have not; schooling is by and large still carried out in ways that were designed to serve an industrial society, ways that have become completely outmoded and counterproductive. The demands placed on individuals in a postindustrial era are vastly different from those placed on individuals during the centuries of the industrial era. Our current postindustrial world, according to Greenberg, has no need for people who are like "cogs in a machine." Nor is it any longer necessary for people to know the sort of things that, during the past few centuries, were assumed essential, such as reading and mathematics. Technology can now do many things human beings used to do.

What *is* needed, the Sudbury Valley School staff believes, are people who are creative, take responsibility, exercise judgment, and make decisions for themselves. In order for a school to serve this cultural need it would have to do the following things: "allow for a tremendous amount of diversity … allow people to become, on their own, self-starters, initiators, entrepreneurs … allow children to grow up completely at home with the cultural values of our country, especially such essential values as tolerance, mutual respect, and self-government" (Greenberg, 1992, p. 224).

One characteristic of the shift from industrial to postindustrial society that is important in the Sudbury Valley School rejection of curriculum is the transformation in model-building (Greenberg, 1992). During the industrial era, the way in which people made sense of the world and solved problems was to build mental models that were based in the modernist dichotomy of subjective and objective and appealed to distinctions between art, science, philosophy, history, and so on. The postindustrial era, Greenberg says, is characterized by *unfettered, or free-form, model-building* (p. 95) . Abandoning the conventions that define and categorize intellectual disciplines frees one to engage in mental pursuits dominated by imagination, rather than by systematic application of rules. Concepts once reserved for art (as distinct from science), "such as beauty, spirit, and appropriateness, weave in and out of every creation of the mind" (p. 95). In a postindustrial culture, "life is an *art form*, in the broadest understanding of that term" (p. 97).

Play is important in the Sudbury Valley School educational model because of its role in free-form, model-building activity. The common connotation of play as having no practical use is not being invoked here; rather, it is play as creative and exploratory. According to Greenberg, children's play is a form of free-form, model-building activity. He argues, therefore, that child's play not be reserved for early childhood but should be encouraged for an extended period of time. Play—the imaginative experimentation with alternative constructs, the rearrangement of existing structures into new ones—needs to be the dominant free-form, model-building activity at all stages of life in postindustrial society. Here and elsewhere, when Greenberg and other Sudbury Valley School staff speak of play, they are referring to "mental play" as in "playing with ideas."

Sudbury Valley School calls age-mixing its "secret weapon" (Greenberg, 1987, p. 96). The school is structured to allow people of different ages to mix freely with one another. This feature of the school is one that I find most attractive because (to use Vygotskian language) such heterogeneity can create overlapping ZPDs and is, thereby, potentially developmental. Greenberg and I, although from very different philosophical perspectives and discourse traditions, tend toward a shared perspective on the value of age-mixing. Greenberg believes that segregating children by age or so-called developmental level is both artificial and harmful. Schools might be unique as a major cultural institution where people of different ages, abilities and interests do not mix (freely or not).

Both the home and the workplace (the two places aside from schools where people in industrial and postindustrial societies spend the bulk of their time) depend on a continuous intermingling of people who differ in these and other ways. According to Greenberg (1987), from the ways adults ordinarily go about their business, it must be considered positive for adults with different degrees of experience in life and work to have contact and to communicate with one another (p. 98). This is one way that we learn—by seeing how other people approach problems and carry out their activities. It is reasonable to think, then, that creating environments in which there are diverse alternatives (including successful models) would be particularly vital for young children, given their limited abilities and skills.

Greenberg (1987) discussed the harm done in denying these kinds of opportunities to children. On the one hand, learning from adults is often difficult for children because, as models, adults can be "too far away" (i.e., so advanced as to be beyond the reach of the child). On the other hand, grouping children by age (or, what is worse to Greenberg, by developmental level) puts them in a situation where they have no successful models—they are all in the same boat, so to speak. The traditional school structure combines the worst of these extremes—"take a bunch of children at the same developmental age and then stick them in a room together with an adult" (p. 104). What is lost are the enormously rich possibilities that exist when there is a continuum of diversity, when there are many potential models and possibilities for others to serve as a bridge between children and adults. In Vygotskian terms, what is lost is the potential for creative imitation and completion that simultaneously are and create overlapping ZPDs where *learning leads development.*

It is when we examine what other people might be models *for* that Sudbury Valley's philosophy and mine diverge. Greenberg's view was reality-based and mentalistic, while mine is relation-based and activistic. Age-mixing is important at Sudbury because, it is claimed, it aids children in their basic task: to individually and on their own build a mental model of reality, come to grips with the world, and solve problems (Greenberg, 1987, pp. 104–105). Thus, "the other" can serve as a model and catalyst for what is essentially individualized and internal mental process; "the other" can help "the self" learn. In contrast, I take learning to be social, relational activity. As such, learning does not sometimes require "the other"—it entails "the other." Creative imitation and completion, the critical elements that create the ZPD, as Vygotsky told us, are made manifest the more heterogeneous the environmental elements out of which the ZPD is built.

The language of Sudbury Valley School, which I have attempted to replicate, is devoid of postmodern conceptions—there is no talk of modernism or postmodernism, deconstruction, the sociology of knowledge, narrative, or voice. At the same time, both its philosophy and success over nearly 30 years arise from what can be identified as postmodern concerns. An historical review of philosophy of education by Smeyers and Marshall (1995) helps to locate Sudbury Valley School's approach in contemporary intellectual traditions. In their introduction to *Philosophy and Education: Accepting Wittgenstein's Challenge,* Smeyers and Marshall framed the educational implications of the claim that modernity has come to an end in this way: "The question as to why schools aren't doing their 'job' anymore becomes instead the question can schools, within the traditional and 'given' conceptual framework, do their job at all?" (p. 28). In my view, the Sudbury Valley School model is an answer in practice to this second question.

Smeyers and Marshall (1995) charted the historical landscape of postmodern schools of thought in philosophy of education. For example, they distinguished the *anti-pedagogy* approach in the following way: "As knowledge can no longer be claimed to be applicable to a rapidly changing future, it is argued, the justification of present educational activities is called into question. For some philosophers of education this suspicion evolves into a full condemnation of all pedagogy" (p. 31). This aptly describes Sudbury Valley's practice—more a rejection or negation of pedagogy than a positive creation of a new educational method. Given how harmful schooling can be to children, an educational environment that is self-consciously structured so as to minimize harm, to my way of thinking, has much to offer. Being "anti-pedagogy" myself, I might have done exactly what Greenberg and his colleagues have done, had I not discovered Vygotsky and been mentored in methodology by Newman.[1]

From the relational, activity–theoretic, nonepistemological perspective, Sudbury Valley School is potentially developmental in not being learning-centered. The lack of constraints on creative activity, coupled with the demand for personal and collective responsibility (via participatory democracy), creates infinite possibilities for learning to lead development. Its philosophy, however, is less than developmental; in theory, it is not a nonepistemological, therapeutic modality. The foundational units of modernism—the logic of the particular, the isolated individual located in a dualistically divided world, the primacy of mental processes—are not even opened up for questioning, much less abandoned. Some of the substantive accoutrements of the epistemological paradigm are rejected (although not deconstructed). But modernism's ontology—the self, (self-) knowledge, the mind—are embraced.

GROWING AT SUDBURY VALLEY

Earlier, I referred to Sudbury Valley School's ongoing process of self-evaluation. It is helpful to examine this work relative to its break with the epistemological paradigm.

In addition to the usual informal ways private schools try to keep up with alumni, Sudbury Valley School has conducted an oral history project (Sadofsky & Greenberg, 1994) and four follow-up studies of former students (in 1972, 1975, 1981–1982, and 1991). The 1991 study, entitled *Legacy of Trust: Life After the Sudbury Valley School Experience* (Greenberg & Sadofsky, 1992), includes many personal comments by former students as well as extensive quantitative data. The authors, both long-time staff members, state their multiple purposes in conducting the study: "A school like Sudbury Valley,

---

[1]The key players in the formation of the Sudbury Valley School and the community of which the Barbara Taylor School is a part have crossed paths over the years. The first time was in 1967 when the school was being formed by Dan and Hanna Greenberg and seven others. Among the many people who had heard about the school and were briefly involved was Fred Newman. In a personal account of the beginning of Sudbury Valley School, Greenberg (1973) described a meeting that was pivotal for the democratic shape the school was to take, and recounts the role Newman played in advocating for full inclusion and openness.

Twenty-five years passed. In 1992, Greenberg and I met when we both were presenters at a conference/retreat of the ERIS Society in Aspen, Colorado. That we wound up meeting there says something about the independent and nonideological stance of both Sudbury Valley School and the developing development community I had been building all those years. For ERIS was by no means a left or even liberal outfit; present at that retreat were "innovative thinkers" from all over the political spectrum and every discipline, from Greenberg and me to Mormons, cybernetics experts, physicists, Scientologists, and healers. Since then, we have visited each other's schools and been in regular communication.

based on principles that are radical departures from those that underlie the prevailing educational models, is more motivated than most schools to have answers" (pp. 7–8) to questions about its effectiveness, success, and drawbacks. They were concerned, understandably, to determine if attending Sudbury Valley in any way reduced a person's options later in life. In addition, they hoped the study would "serve as a starting point for examining some expectations we have had about the [positive] influence a Sudbury Valley education may have on students who experience it for varying lengths of time, at different parts of their lives" (p. 9).

The study was based on responses to a questionnaire given to former Sudbury Valley students. (Students were sent the questionnaire and responses were recorded during a follow-up telephone interview with a school representative.) The authors were interested in what these young adults were doing now—where they lived, what work they did, if they had pursued higher education, their marital status, and so on—and how they thought about their quality of life and their Sudbury Valley School experience. The study was limited to students who met the following criteria: they had attended the school for at least one year; they had graduated from or left the school after the age of 9; and they were at least 20 years old and had been out of school for at least 2 years at the time of the interview. The analysis is based on 183 students (a 79% response rate), most of whom entered Sudbury during their teens and remained there for 3 to 4 years. Primarily public school students—only 5% to 7% had previously attended a private school—most of them held part-time jobs while at Sudbury.

Much of the analysis compares groups of students based on the length of time they spent at Sudbury Valley and whether they left at high school graduation age or earlier. These data are not the focus of the present discussion. It is worth noting, however, that the percentage of students who received college or university degrees was highest for those whose only school was Sudbury (52%) and lowest for those who attended Sudbury for only 1 year (39%). More significant is that overall, 87% of all former students had some formal postsecondary schooling. In addition, none of the respondents were unemployed. The largest percentages worked in managerial positions, various trades and crafts, and education.

The qualitative data—many brief comments and several lengthy self-reflections—suggest that former Sudbury students are relatively happy with their vocational choices, get gratification from their work, and find their lives interesting. Many of them attribute their ability to learn and know what they want out of life to their school experience. For example, a 24-year-old photographer and owner of a crafts cafe had this to say:

> I learned how to write at Sudbury Valley, and then freshman year in college, I had to take writing. I had to write a research paper. I said to myself, "I know how to do that. No problem." I had prepared myself. I definitely hadn't prepared myself for the math

that they bombarded me with the first year, but I struggled through. It was another case of, well, here's the material, yes, I can learn this if I have to ... I learned about art, about literature, and the sciences when I was younger.... Sudbury Valley was a good school and it was an enjoyable place to grow up because you grew up academically and socially and physically all at the same time. It didn't come in stages. I realize more and more each year what I got from the school. (Greenberg & Sadofsky, 1992, p. 86)

Other students echoed or expanded on her comments:

I got into music at Sudbury Valley. I learned to play guitar by just playing. I had the time to do what I really loved. Now I am one of a group of 30 musicians who form different bands playing all kinds of music at all sorts of occasions. I love my work. (p. 131)

[Before Sudbury Valley] I hadn't understood that I was a really intellectual kind of person. I didn't know that at all. I went from an environment where everything was superficial and weird and hard to understand, to understanding a little about what kind of person I was, a lot more about what kind of a world it really is and sort of being able to analyze how to go about getting the things I wanted out of my life and out of the community, and contribute at the same time. (p. 144)

If you've been to Sudbury Valley, you realize that this stuff has to get done, and you chose to work there and get it done. So even if you can't stand your boss, you realize you have to get it done. You're not at a disadvantage because you never had a boss in school. (p. 47)

Sudbury Valley helped me to liberate my concepts. I read more and problem solved more than in public school. I learned what and when I wanted without pressure. It helped me a lot. (p. 180)

Interestingly, Greenberg and Sadofsky (1992) stated at the beginning of the book that they do not know the significance of these kinds of comments. They speculate that the former students might have been overwhelmingly positive because the caller was a school representative and these young adults felt they had to be polite and say nice things. On the other hand, maybe they wanted to present *themselves* in a favorable light. Or, perhaps they simply had nothing negative to say (p. 12). I find this little disclaimer curious in light of the Sudbury Valley philosophy. Although it is obvious that the authors take the unsolicited comments by former students to be of great interest, they are loathe (or at least conflicted about whether) to consider them as valid data because they dealt with opinions, feelings, and beliefs rather than "factual information." On the one hand, they say that they consciously designed the study to avoid "questions that dealt with the opinions, character traits or beliefs of the respondents" and, further, that this kind of material "will have to be left to studies conducted by persons not associated in any way with the school community" (p. 11). On the other hand, they tell us in the next sentence that "we feel that the compiled data presented in this book gives, in those areas which were investigated, a valid picture ... in no way dependent on the fact that this study was sponsored by the school" (p. 11). If "compiled data" refers only to the tabulated responses to questions, then clearly the unsolicited comments are not considered valid; if "compiled data" is meant to include the comments, then the conditions of the study appear to be violated.

The subtext of Greenberg and Sadofsky's discussion of data here, as I read it, is a concern with objectivity. The distinction between objective and subjective knowledge, and the primacy of objective knowledge are nowhere in the Sudbury Valley School philosophy, nor are they obvious in its day-to-day practice. They are, however, clearly at work here in its conception of evaluation. Why is the fact that the study was sponsored by the school presumed to have a bearing on subjective statements, but not on the "factual information" given? Why are the ways they speak of their lives and their school experience not considered critical to forming "a valid picture of former students?" The same authors have written hundreds of pages insisting on personal responsibility and trust as both the goals of education and what they themselves never waver from giving to and fostering in their students. They have been similarly prolific in railing against the "normal" practice of making claims about students from "factual information." Why this seeming lapse in philosophical consistency?

In pondering this, I am reminded of my first impressions of Sudbury Valley as a "haven in a heartless world." I think the wavering from some of the school's deepest convictions reveals a cynicism and mistrust about the possibility of collective social transformation—an unspoken assumption that the creation of havens is the best we can do. There is a thread of isolationism and utopianism running through writings on the Sudbury Valley School model. The school is portrayed as somehow not *of* this world, but as, in Greenberg's words, "a school *for* the real world" (Greenberg, 1987, p. 13). In seeing their project in this way, the school's founders, intentionally or not, reject the possibility of revolutionary activity—relational activity that produces developmental environments *and* the development such environments support.

Ironically, it might be Sudbury Valley's adherence to individualism that produces this denigration of voice and momentary abandonment of the integrity of personhood. As was discussed earlier, psychology's commitment to self-contained individuals creates (and requires) the subjective–objective split, an inner world and outer reality, a "real" world from which to judge (whenever possible) the truth value of what is said. Apparently, only the objective data can be confidently determined to be true. Rejecting the subjective data, ironically, imposes the criteria of objectivity on what is—within the Sudbury Valley philosophy—ultimately subjective: the Sudbury Valley School experience.

The authors are, in effect, accounting for Sudbury Valley's success by appealing to changes in individuals' mental states (attitudes and aptitudes) as "caused by" the noncoercive and nurturing environment the students were "in." What I find problematic about this is that it denies the fact that it is *they who created this environment*. Becoming who they are by participating in creating their learning environment is neither subjective nor objective; it is relational. And it is this relational, revolutionary activity of transforming schooling, learning, and development—as far as I can tell, the ongoing activity at Sudbury—that, in my view, accounts for its effectiveness. To the extent that it is a haven in a heartless world, it stultifies growth. To the extent that it is, in contrast, "a heart in a havenless world" (Newman, 1991a)—a continuously evolving, inclusive community in a stagnated, overly regimented culture—it is developmental.

Chapter 7

The Barbara Taylor School:
A Development Community
Where Children Learn

◆ ◆ ◆

PERFORMANCE, PLAY, AND IMPROVISATION

Justin[1] (age 11) was lying still on the rug, surrounded by several children and an adult kneeling beside him peering at his bare stomach (his shirt had been hiked up to his neck). Len, the adult learning director, was holding a cylindrical piece of paper upright above Justin's belly button. Caught by the scene and the children's rapt attention, I asked what was happening. "We're performing an operation," they told me, "the surgical removal of immaturity."

Later that day, Justin and Len performed a commercial break during a circus scene created by Alice (age 8) and Julia, another learning director. Len and Justin entered the stage walking. Len said, "Justin, you won't be going to your speech therapist today." Justin stopped in his tracks, yelled, cried, and fell to the ground in a screaming temper tantrum. Len looked up at the audience for a moment, took some wads of paper out of the manila envelope he was holding and said, while he arched them toward Justin's mouth, "The miracle cure—'Matchore Partz' [Mature Parts]." Justin "swallowed the pills." He stood up and he and Len began the scene again. Len: "Justin, you won't be going to your speech therapist today." Justin looked up at him and calmly said, "Oh well, I guess I'll go home then." The audience applauded.

For years, Justin had been having temper tantrums in situations similar to the one improvised in the commercial for "Matchore Partz." Diagnosed with a variety of specific and general learning disabilities and emotional

---

[1]The names of children and adults in this and subsequent scenes have been changed.

problems, Justin had been in special education schools until he entered the Barbara Taylor School at the end of the last school year. His parents were concerned that he had "reached a plateau," as they had heard often happens with children like Justin, and that he just was not developing any further.

Justin is a performer. We all are. Performing is how we learn and develop. What I mean by performing is far closer to how the word is used in theater than in manufacturing; we are not talking here about alienated output. (The recent trend in education of delineating "performance outcomes" is as foreign to what I mean by performance as test scores and grades.) It is through performance—that is, doing what is beyond us (if only for that moment)—that when we are very young children we learn to do the varied things we do not know how to do. As Vygotsky described so eloquently, babies transform from babblers to speakers of a language through performing. The relational activity of creatively imitating others is simultaneously the performance of themselves. Performing is a way of taking "who we are" and creating something new—in this case, a new speaker—through incorporating "the other."

Ironically, as we perform our way into cultural and societal adaptation, we also perform our way out of continuous development. What we have learned (through performing) becomes routinized and rigidified into behavior. We become so skilled at acting out roles that we no longer keep performing. We develop an identity as "this kind of person"—someone who does certain things and feels certain ways. Anything other than that, most of us think, would not be "true" to "who we are." Justin's emotional development was at a standstill; he repeatedly did what he knew how to do—have a tantrum. Like most of us, Justin was unaware that this emotional response (perhaps to frustration, change, or disappointment) was and is jointly and socially constructed by himself and others. It did not (perhaps would not and could not, for whatever reasons) occur to him that there is an infinite number of things one can do or say upon hearing that the plans have changed.

Creating an environment for Justin to perform—both his tantrum and something other than a tantrum—can reinitiate developmental activity. From a Vygotskian perspective, it supports him to go beyond himself, to socially create other responses, to experience being other than who he is, to produce something new, to develop. It breaks the pattern. It challenges the cardinal rule of psychology's "hidden curriculum" —that our actions follow from how we feel. (But if this were really the case, there could be no such thing as theater or other cultural entertainment. Depressed actors would act depressed on stage regardless of the play in which they were performing.) From a Wittgensteinian perspective, performing helps to free Justin of the "picture that holds us captive" (the one way of seeing things). Performing changes his location and relationship to his emotions and is a way of "moving around about" his so-called emotional state (which, in effect, has become a form of alienation) and helps him to create, with others, new emotional forms of life. Justin's performing creates a changed environment (which, in dialectical fashion, is inseparable from him and others) and rekindles his capacity to be a social maker of meaning. The difference between Justin performing his temper tantrum and his typical behavior of having a temper tantrum is the difference between developing and not developing.

The Barbara Taylor School is performatory with its dominant activity, like the scene just described, improvisational performance. The cultural–performatory, nonepistemological, therapeutic approach to understanding human life discussed in chapter 4 is both the basis of the school's practice and a specific expansion of it. The idea is simple to articulate (but exceedingly difficult to practice consistently). Children become successful learners through performing as learners. To perform, you need a performatory environment (often a stage). If the existing environment is not conducive to performance, then it must be reshaped into one that is performatory. Not once, but continuously.

As social institutions go, schools are among the least conducive to performance; they are, typically, nonperformatory and even antiperformatory in structure and ambiance. For example, beyond kindergarten, play (including pretend play, a type of performance in my sense of the term) is discouraged and even disallowed. The dichotomy work/play that is operative in the broader culture is not only strongly reinforced within schools ("stop playing around and get down to work") but is replicated in the dichotomy learning/playing that traditional schools construct organizationally and discursively. For example, in most schools a specific time is set aside for play (at least in the early grades; junior high and high schools often have no play time but "study hall" and physical education classes instead). We speak of doing *school work,* not *school play;* we play *house* but we do not play *reading.*

In spite of the recognition that play is critical in children's development and learning (as many psychologists, e.g., Bruner, Jolly, & Sylva, 1976, and Sutton-Smith, 1976, have long argued persuasively), schools are becoming not more playful but less so. As Rust (1993) noted in a study of kindergartens, far from it being the case that early childhood practices have had a positive influence on elementary school education, the reverse is becoming the norm:

> In the kindergarten, the focus was the "whole child." There was time for play, and play was understood to be the child's work ... Readiness for school came as a by-product of the kindergarten experience ... Where once there was a sense of freedom with regard to the curriculum, now there is pressure on parents and early childhood teachers to make sure that children are ready for school even before they get there. Screening for kindergarten is commonplace, and testing of kindergartners is almost routine. (pp. 4–5)

Thus, children are socialized very early on to associate playing with free time, fun and frivolity, and learning with work, what is important and what is real. So are adults. (If you are a teacher or parent, listen to yourself over the course of a day and hear how you talk to your students or children about school, work, play, and learning.) Even Barbara Taylor School parents, who have consciously chosen a play(performance)-oriented educational environment, can be decidedly uncomfortable when their children respond to the perennial question, "What did you do in school today?" with "We played."

It seems to me that no small part of what is "wrong" with play has to do with our strong cultural commitment to reality and the family of conceptions associated with it, including truth, fact, correctness, and rightness. The dominant mode of instruction is designed to help students "get it right" (the liberal pronouncement "There is no right answer; I just want to know what you think" notwithstanding). Teaching children to get it right (regardless of how practically useful and desirable this may be) is, simultaneously, teaching them that there is something identifiable as truth. It is teaching them to "tell the truth"—about numbers, words on a page, the Civil War, or the shooting down the block. The 3-year-old's scribble of the family dog towering over the family house (both barely recognizable) is applauded; when children are very young we encourage their imagination and care little about reality. By the age of 10, however, this child will get little praise for drawing unrealistically.

I am not arguing against learning about representational art or perspective. What I am concerned with is the manner in which we adapt children to a culture that places such a high premium on reality, truth-telling, and facts. The way the truth-telling game (in Wittgenstein's sense of language-game) is played, the way school talk is accomplished, belies that it is a game or a way of speaking. On the contrary, it reinforces a belief in the existence of truth and a correspondence between "what is true" and something called reality. (This is known in philosophical circles as the correspondence theory of truth; the proposition "It is snowing" is said to be true if and only if it is snowing.) Truth and reality are among the most deeply entrenched ideological components of Western thought; over hundreds of years they have come to define what knowledge, understanding, and meaning are. As mentioned earlier, they are currently under intense scrutiny by critical and postmodern theorists. In relation to curriculum reforms, for example, exposing the lie in the supposed truth "Columbus discovered America" is necessary and valuable for exposing how ideological curricula can be. However, the ideology runs deeper than the class, race, and gender bias of any particular proposition. In order for the ideological bias to be thoroughly exposed, it is necessary to deconstruct the concept of truth itself. After all, identifying a proposition as a lie is meaningful only if there is another proposition presumed to be true. As valuable as it is as a reform, exposing the lies in received history leaves truth-referential epistemology unexamined.

What is so wonderful about play and performance to me is that they subvert Truth and truth-telling. The presumed truth value utterances have in ordinary discourse is suspended in performatory activity. For example, the statement, "My name is Lois," uttered in conversation carries a presumption of truth value (people think, or think they know, that I am either telling the truth or lying). But when a character in a play utters the line, "My name is Cinderella" no one questions its truth value. (No audience member gets up and says, "No you're not! You're my daughter!") Or when a 5-year-old girl says, "I'm the Daddy and you're the baby" in pretend play with her 8-year-old sister, there is no presumption of truth or falsity.

That truth is not a relevant feature of the human activity of performance is one of its most interesting characteristics (as it is in children's free and pretend play). Over the course of history, the human capacity to conceptualize and make abstractions has proved to be remarkably useful. Two of the most significant conceptual abstractions of Western culture are truth and reality, for they have contributed to producing extraordinary advances in science and technology. The questions being raised about them (here and in much of postmodern literature) have to do with their applicability to human learning and their relevance to the continued development of our species. After all, 2-year-olds manage quite well without being held accountable for the truth, indeed, without having any awareness of it at all. They learn and develop at a fantastic rate, participating in life activities with their families and caregivers in an environment that is, to a large extent, unconstrained by truth-referentiality. Might there be a lesson here? Might we question whether we need Truth? Might it be the case that its uncritical acceptance has come to hinder us in all sorts of ways including, paradoxically, in the learning of "truth-telling" itself? In my view, the suspension and subversion of Truth is no small part of what makes performance and pretend play so growthful and why a performatory approach to learning can rekindle development.

THE SCHOOL'S HISTORY

When the Barbara Taylor School was founded in Harlem, New York in 1985, two progressive traditions—that of African-American community schools and the (mostly White) free school movement—came together. Two years earlier, Barbara Taylor, the founder and principal of the St. Thomas Community School in Harlem, met the Institute for Social Therapy and Research (the form and name of the developing development community during most of the 1980s). At that time, the Institute developed, practiced, and trained people in social therapy, and implemented several projects that utilized this developmental methodology in the areas of health, education, and culture. At 62, Taylor had already enjoyed a long career as a successful and dedicated educator—she had been an elementary school teacher, reading specialist, assistant principal, principal, and founder of a community school. Courageous and energetic, Taylor had been guided in her professional life by her commitment to helping poor children learn and grow. As principal of the St. Thomas School—which operated under the auspices of the archdiocese of New York—she led a group of parents in a prolonged fight against the Church bureaucracy when it decided to withdraw regular funding from the school after Taylor had successfully raised supplementary funds. The result was the formation of the independent St. Thomas Community School, with Taylor as principal.

After several years, Taylor felt that St. Thomas' organization as a dynamic community school had gone as far as it could. She felt she needed a new methodology with which to build a school environment where children would be challenged and supported to be successful learners, the kind of fabulous learners they are in the preschool years. Taylor believed that the Institute had some valuable things to offer her: a shared social vision; a methodology for building and our experiences as community organizers; the practice of social therapy; and a network of progressive people from a variety of class, professional, and ethnic backgrounds who could support her. Our collaboration began.

During its first 6 years, the Barbara Taylor School concentrated on creating conditions for children to be emotionally supported and challenged in order to be able to learn. Much hard work was done to "Stop Abusive Behavior Syndrome"—minimizing the kinds of (nonphysical) abuse that are routine in schools, such as the way adults humiliate students and students humiliate one another, the standard practice of teaching to tests with no regard for the learning process, an insistence on following rules that have to do only with control, and the classism, racism, sexism, and homophobia that are ingrained in schools and teaching practices. Taylor herself led this work by asking the students to share how she was abusive to them; one way, they told her, was "that" look she gave them. From there, discussions moved to how students were abusive to her, other staff, and to one another. Students and teachers created a variety of improvisational activities and policies out of these conversations as responses to the question, "What can/should we do about abuse?" No small part of the success of this project was the willingness of the staff to take risks and be ready to hear what the students had to say. What was inseparable from this was their skill in organizing the environment for this to happen.

During these years, the school utilized a standard curriculum in innovative ways. Geared toward "developing children as leaders," the school supported the students' active participation and their activism. Much classwork was interdisciplinary; peer teaching and older students tutoring younger students were regular features of the school day; and the student body was often in the courtroom or marching in demonstrations for human and civil rights. The school was successful. Barbara Taylor School students' achievement scores on standardized tests exceeded those of public school students in the district—and they learned without being coerced or abused. (See LaCerva, 1992, and Strickland & Holzman, 1989, for discussions of this phase in the life of the Barbara Taylor School.)

This alone, we believed, was a significant accomplishment. We were, however, eager to develop the approach further in a Vygotskian direction which, to us, meant to create the school as a continuously emerging environment where learning leads development—not *a* (ZPD) but *many* ZPDs. Our reading of Vygotsky led us to believe that many ever-changing and overlapping ZPDs have to be created and that it is through this relational, creative activity that people learn developmentally. We felt that the standard practices of grouping students by age (although Barbara Taylor School students were divided into three groups—kindergarten–Grade 2, Grades 3–5, and Grades 6–8) and following a curriculum might constrain the continuous creation of ZPDs. The transition of the Barbara Taylor School into a Vygotskian laboratory began in September 1991. We provocatively called our approach Children Helping to Educate Another Training (CHEAT; see Holzman, 1993, for a description of CHEAT).

The Barbara Taylor School laboratory was housed on one floor of a Harlem brownstone from 1991 until it relocated to a Brooklyn storefront in November 1994. With 20 students, ages 4 to 14, and three full-time staff there each day, and a principal, director, administrator, volunteers, interns, guest teachers, and parents coming and going during the week, it was a "postmodern" one-room schoolhouse. Following Vygotsky, we have spoken of our collective work as dealing with "the tasks raised by history" in the course of living together each day; in this sense, our activity is revolutionary (Vygotsky, cited on p. 23). It is, in this sense, also therapeutic and developmental.

Hardly a week would go by without a visit from a psychologist, educator, or university student from somewhere in the world. (Our most honored guest was Lev Vygotsky's daughter, Gita Vygodskaya—herself a psychologist.) Their entrance is never formal. Rather, they are invited to join the ongoing improvisational activities, bringing their expertise, interest, and curiosity to what the students happen to be doing. Three to four times a month there is a school trip. Some are planned, such as the chamber music concert series at Lincoln Center and the art history series at the Brooklyn Museum; others are suggested and organized by the students in the course of the year, for example, a visit to a homeopath and health food store. Occasionally, students from other schools spend the day at the Barbara Taylor School, for example, a group of "school refusers" from a Japanese alternative school and a special education class from a Harlem public school. During 1996, a volunteer teacher project was launched—Children Having the Opportunity to Invite Community Educators (CHOICE). Month-long courses were offered by a diverse group of professionals (including architects, doctors, artists, actors, chefs, and social scientists) who had something they wanted to teach to the students. These classes were held at a second site a few blocks away from the school.

CHARACTERISTICS OF DEVELOPMENTAL LEARNING

The structure of the Barbara Taylor School comes into being simultaneously with its activities. It is *improvisational, activity-centered, and radically democratic*. Being a student or a staff member is both liberating and demanding, for there is no curriculum to follow, no set schedule, no fixed divisions of students. (The only constant is "strike"—as in "strike the set"—which occurs before lunch, after lunch, and at the end of the school day when children and adults put things away, wash the dishes, sweep the floor, vacuum the rug, clean the bathrooms, and sort the garbage and trash for recycling, all directed in their parts by a weekly strike director.) Each day, the students and adults decide, together, what they will do. The task of the learning directors (they are called that and not teachers because they function much like theater directors) is to lead the students and each other in the creative, relational activity of creating a developmental learning environment—performing the school anew each day. They must perform beyond themselves as directors of continuously emergent improvisational life scenes rather than behave as teachers, disciplinarians, or even facilitators of learning. Their responsibility is to create potentially developmental situations by bringing their expertise as learners, discoverers, risk takers, writers, scientists, and musicians into ongoing activities. Rather than beginning with a preconceived notion of learning and imposing it (either through explicit coercion or child-centered manipulations), the learning directors encourage students to perform ahead of themselves (to create their learning) and then support them in whatever they wind up doing.

The following vignette, written by a learning director, illustrates one way this kind of activity-centered learning and improvisational "lesson" can look.

Kevin [age 7] and I were sitting on the floor next to each other in the quiet room. I put two of my fingers in the palm of his hand and asked him to guess what number. He said two. I asked him if he knew by looking; he said, "No, I closed my eyes." Then we started talking about how blind people read. I said blind people use their fingers to read, explaining the concept of Braille and telling him that it was paper that had bumps on it. I thought of getting some paper to make a Braille book but things didn't go that way. Instead, Rafael [age 7], who had overheard us, started walking in the corridor with his eyes closed, pretending he was blind. Kevin and some other kids—Kayla [age 6], Alicia [age 5], Chancy [age 6], Joy [age 4], and Matthew [age 4] followed suit.

The conversation between the kids was loud. "I can't see! I'm blind!" "Where are you going? Look out! You're bumping into me!" "I know where I'm going even though I can't see!"

I asked Rafael how he knew where he was going if he couldn't see and he said that he was using his hands to feel where he was going. Then Kevin said he knew which way he was going because he could hear the movie in the next room. The parade of blind kids lasted about 30 seconds. Then they all tumbled into the office and starting fighting "blind" on the couch. I started singing, "Three Blind Mice." Joy got on her knees and started crawling out of the office with her eyes closed. Kayla and Chancy followed, singing along with me. Things got really noisy as kids started wrestling with each other. Carl [age 14] and I decided we would take these kids outside.

Outside, I asked the group what they wanted to play. They started miming baseball: we "pitched," "hit," "ran bases," and "caught the ball" a few times. Then Rafael asked if we could play basketball: "Hey, can we play basketball? I know! Let's play basketball deaf! No talking!"

A rigorous game of deaf basketball ensued. We passed, dribbled, shot baskets and did tricks with imaginary balls while moving around "the court." Rafael told the others a few times that we couldn't talk because we were deaf. After the game fizzled out, the kids played "Ocean Tag" (in which the shark is It) on the slide, making up the game and its rules as they went along.

In this situation, the learning director did not have something specific she wanted to teach (there are times when she does). Her activity with Kevin, and then with the group of children, emerged or came to define itself. She tried to create with what the children were doing rather than insisting that they do what she intended (even if her intention was only seconds old). Her introduction of Braille was not developed, as a student went somewhere else with being blind (pretending to be blind). Abandoning her idea to make a Braille book, she drew the students' attention to their other senses as they pretended to be blind; she brought something to what they were doing. Rather than scolding them for fighting, she related to them "in character," building on their performance by introducing "Three Blind Mice."

What were the children learning? This is a most reasonable sounding question, but I think it is unanswerable, not only in this situation but in traditional, formal lesson situations as well. Do we know what children are learning when they, for example, are in science class and told the definitions of the five senses or, in a more hands-on class, *instructed* to imagine what it is like to be blind or deaf? To my way of thinking, it is the systematic nature of these lessons (including that they are conceived of beforehand and come complete with specific goals and objectives) that leads us to think we know what children are learning from them. What if, however, learning is unsystematic? Moreover, what if thinking we need to know what is learned actually interferes with learning?

It is our belief that learning that leads and constantly contributes to development is, in fact, unsystematic and unknowable (in the usual sense of *knowing about*). Although we can always find a pattern in life's continuously emerging scenes, and although we can always impose a systematic and rule-governed interpretation on them, Wittgenstein asked us to consider whether this is a form of mythology, whether explanations and abstract generalizations, in fact, distort life. Human development and learning—as relational activities—do not require understanding (i.e., cognition and appraisal). This is our claim. Developmental learning is unsystematic, in the sense that it is best understood in terms of itself—as a form of life—rather than in terms of (any) models of science and reason. As a practice of method that offers possibilities for people to participate in whatever ways and to whatever extent they choose, it is—from our understanding of what is most human about Vygotsky's psychology and Wittgenstein's philosophy—developmental.

The radically democratic nature of the Barbara Taylor School goes beyond the participatory, parliamentary structure of the Sudbury Valley School. Although we do collectively set policy and occasionally vote on issues, these actions are taken as part of the overall and continuous activity of creating an environment of inclusion. We struggle to practice democracy as developmental activity. To us, radical democracy refers to the collective activity of people *governing and transforming themselves*. The Barbara Taylor School is democratic to the extent that creating the school is inclusionary and voluntary, not to the extent that rules institutionalizing democratic process are followed.

This means that the bases for decisions include what is supportive of the school and everyone's development. If a student wants to study dinosaurs all year or has been spending a lot of time at the computer or playing the piano, whether she continues to do what she is doing is determined by what she and others think about it, including whether they think it supports the school's development. Notions of fairness and what is normal (such as a notion of what "a child her age" should be doing in school) inevitably come up in such discussions, often taking the conversation in fascinating directions. Radical democracy also means to us that students are urged to be creative in how they and their fellow students go about learning. It also means that anyone—child or adult—can call a meeting at any time to discuss an issue. It is our belief that it is the *process* of creating an environment in which a 4-year-old can hold the floor and be heard and respected in a mixed-age and heterogenous group that is most valuable.

The challenge and responsibility of this approach is to use what each person has to give—not only their interests and strengths but also their limitations and perceived problems—to create developmental learning. There are more efficient ways to deal with a student prone to temper tantrums (like Justin) than encouraging the student body to figure out (discover, create) new ways of relating that do not define him as a problem. But it is this difficult work—the process of creating the environment for discovery inseparable from the discovery—that maximizes the transformative potential of the experience. Similarly, helping an eighth grader prepare for high school by setting up a school within the school (the students called it "P. S. No Number") can be growthful as a self-conscious reshaping of the existing environment into a collective effort to "produce the prepared graduate."

It is the ongoing relational activity of the group, not the behavior of the individual child, that is the tool-and-result of developmental learning. We believe that the "unit" that learns developmentally is the group. We can phrase it formalistically: *When the group develops, everyone learns. When individuals learn, no one develops.* The development of the group, in Vygotskian terminology, depends on the continuous creation of ZPDs (as was suggested in the educational approach of the Golden Key project). Moreover, Vygotsky's discoveries about the characteristics of the environment of early childhood that supports children to become language makers and language users, when transformed into a nonepistemological, therapeutic modality, suggest a second "axiom" of developmental learning: *We must continuously create the environment even as we learn in it* (Holzman, 1995a, p. 204).

I have claimed that "we are all performers." According to many psychological and anthropological studies and ordinary everyday observation, children seem to be performers par excellence. Would that it followed in life that children enthusiastically embraced performance as a way to do school! By far the greatest difficulty in the Barbara Taylor School's radical educational model is the resistance to performance. The dilemma is that the youngest children perform "naturally" and many older children relate to performance as "stupid" or "silly." Because adults tend to remain outsiders to young children's play, it is a challenge to bring something to what they are doing when, in a most fundamental way, they are doing exactly what you want them to be doing! And adults, often conflicted about older children's desire to look cool, can find it difficult to break through their "attitude." As well-trained in and committed to performance as the staff are, they can all too easily back down from performing the school in the face of this kind of resistance and their desire to nurture the caring, but very complex, relationships that they have with the students. Many a staff training has been spent talking about the fact that some students say they "don't like to perform." In what ways is that relevant? Do we presume to know what the students mean when they say that? How do they, as directors, respond? Is there "a performatory response?" What is performance?

As educators who read Vygotsky as a dialectical activity-theorist, we know that we must have an environment conducive to performance in order to perform; the bulk of the work is creating that performatory environment. When some members do not want to perform—or disrupt the environment so that no one can perform—what is to be done? At the Barbara Taylor School, this is often—but never often enough—worked on collectively (sometimes by the whole school, sometimes by the group who are the most involved). Attempts are made to include the nonparticipation, whatever it might look like, in the performance. For example, suppose that an adult or child who is speaking is constantly interrupted. Any number of things can be done. Someone could say, "Okay, let's include in this scene 'the pain in the butt' who keeps bothering us." Or, "Let's all play the interrupting game" (and then everyone talks at once). Or (directed to the person who is interrupting), "If you really can't wait to say what you have to say, then do it as a performance. Do it again, but this time say it louder and with more emotion." Or someone might say, "I need help. So-and-so is getting me mad." Or the group might stop (rather than alter) their performance and talk about what they want to do and how they feel about the interruptions. Sometimes, of course, nothing "works."

We are most eager to create an endless stream of activities in which adults and children alike have the experience of being able to stop what they are doing and create something new out of it, either by doing it again (and perhaps again and again) or doing something entirely different. Being able to "do the scene over again" is, we believe, a critical life experience. For the claim we are making (when we are being theoreticians) is that performing one's life is how we create development.

There have been a few students whose resistance to performing and to taking active responsibility for their learning (environment) was so great that they could not function in the Barbara Taylor School. John, a 10-year old boy who had come from a restricted environment in a public school setting because of physically violent behavior, attended the Barbara Taylor School for 3 months. During this time, the students and staff worked to support him to develop in specific ways: asking for help; creatively imitating others; deciding (as an ongoing process) if he wanted to be at this school; taking responsibility for his actions. The situation was often intense and volatile and, finally, it was his fellow students who raised that he was too disruptive to remain in the school. They said they had worked very hard, tried everything they could think of, and were not willing to continue when it seemed that John did not want their help to develop.

We discussed the gains we had made—the students had learned to not be abusive in response to his abuse, and John himself had developed some new emotional responses. (One example is that early on John had said that the reason he hits is that he wants attention. Others told him there were lots of other things to do when you want attention, including just saying, "I want attention!" The next day John came over to two students and sang "I want attention." After that, he often—but not always—said or sang this instead of hitting someone.) Yet overall, we had collectively failed in being able to maintain a positive total environment. John left the school.

THE FLOW OF (POTENTIALLY)
DEVELOPMENTAL ACTIVITY

Perhaps a description of some of the activities that took place during a particular week at the Barbara Taylor School will give a feel for the life of the school. My description is not an example of a "typical week" to be generalized, but one person's description of specific activities that were created by specific people. To take it as *an example* of what goes on (or as an example of anything) would violate the very spirit of the school. One can always, of course, impose structure, pattern, and generalization on emergent life activities but, more often than not, it is then the structure, pattern, or generalization that one remembers. I think too much is lost through this distortion.

On Monday, a former professional chef now pursuing a master's degree in public health comes to the second site to teach a class in culture, nutrition, and cooking. This is the first of four weekly classes she is offering. Like all the guest teacher classes, this one is voluntary. Eight students, ranging in ages from 5 to 12, take the class. Two learning directors walk the students over and participate themselves in the class.

At the school's main site, five students (ages 9–14) are involved in a game of Jeopardy. Two of them worked for about an hour making up categories, questions and answers, and making play money. They set up a stage in the front of the school, complete with chairs for the audience. The game show was improvised from beginning to end, including two commercial breaks. A 12-year-old girl is sitting at a table by herself, practicing writing in script. Learning director Andrea comes over to do it with her. The two of them and three other students they invited to join them created a writing-in-script game, a form of written "hot potato" in which what was passed along kept changing. First, it was script letters, then script words, then doodles, and then designs. They completed their performance as script writers by telling a one-word story written in script (the story builds by each person giving one word at a time).

In the afternoon, a parent who is a physician at a New York City hospital comes to teach his science class, which has been going on for 5 weeks. Today, three students and one learning director walk the few blocks to attend.

Back at the storefront, two boys, ages 11 and 13, are at a computer. Five children, ages 4 to 6, are under a table with a learning director who is reading them a story. Two 12-year-olds are playing Uno. Five boys and learning director Alan are around the TV learning a new video game. Three youngsters, ages 7 to 9, are involved in building a city and train route.

Rashid, age 14, asks for my help in fundraising for the new computer. He began this project a month ago ("I want the school to have a state-of-the-art computer," he announced). Having called a meeting of the school and obtained agreement, he has written (and rewritten and rewritten again) four different solicitation letters, gotten help from fellow students in preparing a "rap" for his calls to parents and businesses, rehearsed his performance, made the calls, and hung a display on the wall showing monies coming in. Seven hundred dollars has been collected so far from parents, staff, friends, and a few businesses in the community. Rashid says he feels stuck because this is only half the amount needed. He asks if I know any foundations that might contribute to our fund. I suggest he call Donna, an educational psychologist who has visited the school and knows about funding. He asks me if I will do it with him because he is shy. I dial the number for him and he speaks to her quite professionally. He also asks me to make sure that the purchase of the computer and computer education is talked about at the parent–staff meeting later that evening.

Tuesday brings another guest teacher, who is beginning his course in the history of the Black Panthers. An actor who is a former Black Panther, he is eager to share his history with the students. The younger students are interested in attending the class but several of the older ones comment that they "already know everything about the Panthers." When asked what they know, one replies, "They were crazy." They eventually get reorganized to hear someone's first-hand experiences, but the issue of craziness, unfortunately, is not pursued.

Throughout the week, the school continues its test-making and test-taking project. Each spring, the school spends three to four weeks involved in activities designed to demystify tests and testing and help the students become successful test takers. In addition to constructing various kinds of tests themselves, they get practice in taking standardized tests. Over the past 2 weeks, the students have been constructing tests for each other, the staff, and their parents. They have made math, science, music, history, spelling, and reading comprehension tests (sometimes spending hours researching and writing them) and taken them to be xeroxed. Today they take each other's tests. When I arrive at the end of the day for a staff development meeting, several of them greet me excitedly and say, "Where were you? You missed the performance of a lifetime!"

On Wednesday, a fight breaks out between two brothers, ages 6 and 9 (both brand new to the school). A learning director who witnessed it breaks them apart and calls loudly, "Tamal and Charles are fighting—I need some help!" Everyone gathers around, at first those children and adults who are close by, and then everyone after being called. For about 20 minutes the group discusses what to do, what happened, what will help them, and so on. "It's natural. It's a brother thing" one boy says. His brother challenges him, "Well, you don't do that to me." "Charles is new. He doesn't know we don't do that here." "How can he learn it? Can we help him? How did you learn it?" For the first 10 minutes, Charles (the older, and very husky, brother) is cursing loudly and threatening his brother. Children and adults are trying to calm him down and physically restrain him from going after his brother and others, even as the discussion is going on. Once he agrees to sit in a chair and not go after anyone, the conversation focuses on whether brothers "have to" fight and what to do when you're angry. Several students tell Charles what they have learned to do when they are angry and want to hit someone. He is asked if he wants help to do something different with his anger and if he could imitate one of the other students. Some of the students hold firmly to the belief that anger is something that "comes over you" and cannot be controlled; others disagree. A 9-year-old asks Tamal, the younger brother, if he thinks he can ask for help next time Charles hits him instead of kicking his brother. He says he can. When asked if he can ask for help next time, Charles says no. The group breaks up to prepare for lunch.

Charles and two students and two adults continue the discussion for a little while. Charles wants to call his mother and leave, which is something he did often at his other school. We tell him we don't know whether or not he should call her. Obviously, he wants to and that is important. But we urge him to consider other things in making his decision, including his development—could he learn to do other things besides call his mother when he is upset?—his mother, and the school. The suggestion is made that he take a walk with a learning director and think about it for a few minutes. When they return, Charles joins the rest of the group.

During lunch, the students and adults at first speak about brothers and sisters—how many they have, do they fight, what they look like, family resemblances, and why some siblings look alike and others do not. The talk turns to riddles and from there to a game of "What's the opposite of …?"

After lunch, the students "strike" the lunch set and play fight, wrestle, and do simple acrobatics for awhile. Learning directors circulate, making sure each group has "a safety director." Then a learning director makes the announcement, "Five minutes to test taking!" Having taken their self-constructed tests, they will now take "New York State's" tests—samples of standardized tests given to elementary school students in public schools. Len appears with the school camera and asks kids to pose with their "test face" (like the pro athletes' "game face"). He takes individual and group shots until the camera is out of film. The students take seats at different tables. They work absolutely quietly for 90 minutes (except for the youngest students, who are being tested orally). No one says, "No talking."

Thursday begins with a school meeting at which the day is planned. Most of the students want to go to the park because it is finally warm and sunny. A discussion of *how* they will go there ensues—what will their performance be? What began as a matter-of-fact conversation concerning safety (no running, holding hands, and the like) turns into a lengthy conversation about ways of walking, gravity, and weightlessness. Maybe they should be creatures from other planets; how would you walk (or would you walk?) if you were from Jupiter or Mars? They decide to try it, to go to the park in the morning and continue the test-taking performance in the afternoon. It is agreed that the three students who do not wish to go can remain in the school; one boy wants to work on the play he is writing; another wants to play Mathbusters; and a girl wants to look in a science book and the encyclopedia and learn about the universe.

Most of Friday is taken up with a trip to Hostos Community College in the Bronx. An hour's subway ride away, the College hosts a year-long series of cultural events for school children. This day they are seeing a Brazilian dance troupe. After the performance the students talk with the dancers and director and take group snapshots.

LEARNING THAT YOU ARE A LEARNER

Essential to the Barbara Taylor School educational approach as a Vygotskian practice is the importance of relating to children as readers, writers, physicists, geographers, historians, mathematicians, and so on—that is, encouraging them to perform these activities whether or not they "know how"—as the tool-and-result of creating developmental learning and its environment. Elsewhere I have noted that this is especially important with children who have a history of failure to learn in previous schools and classrooms, because such children typically have neither learned very well how to learn nor identify very strongly as learners (Holzman, 1995a). Furthermore, the failure to develop in this way, I believe, is inseparable from the failure to create an environment in which they can perform as learners. In the case of mathematics, for example, repeated attempts to teach the mechanisms of multiplication to a child who is "not good in math" or is "math-phobic"—typically fail "in the absence of creating an environment for the child to perform as a mathematician (to make meaning, to do 'math talk')" (Holzman, 1995a, p. 204).

The following example (Holzman, 1995a) of creating an environment for "math talk" is given in a fair amount of detail in order to invite comparisons with a typical, more structured and goal-directed math lesson. The situation involves a 13-year-old boy, another student and two adults. Two incidents on two consecutive days are presented. The initial interaction consisted of a conversation between the student, David, and learning director Carol about how he had been taught math before, what he learned, what she knew about math and wanted to learn, and who in the school might help them. Early on, Carol asked David how he thought he might learn math and what they could do together. This framed their activity as learners, rather than as knower and nonknower. Carol is not seeking to find out David's developmental level so she can "teach to it." She invites David to create something with her, not to learn mathematics from her separate from that creating.

The second incident occurred the following day:

Carol, David, and Nancy, a 10-year-old girl, are sitting at a table. Carol says she wants to get to know them and is not sure how. Do they have any ideas? They don't. Nancy leaves. Carol and David begin to work on constructing the multiplication tables they began the day before. Nancy returns with a jigsaw puzzle and begins to put it together. The conversation while they are doing these activities is awkward as Carol urges them to tell her something about themselves and David and Nancy are shyly quiet in the face of these "invitations." Nancy asks if she could turn the radio on; Carol says OK, and rap music was added to the environment. David and Nancy begin to talk about the music, lyrics and rap artists. Carol continues to try to "get to know them," telling them some of her reasons and how it isn't easy. She says that she realizes that she does know some things about them—she now knows David likes (name of a rap star). All the while, the conversation among the three of them includes "multiplication talk" ("What's 7 x 6?" "The 5's are easy." "8's are hard. I never remember them.")

I have been observing this scene for a while and come over as David is saying, somewhat judgmentally, that Nancy isn't doing math. Carol says she is not so sure of that; how does he know she's not? He says, "because she's just doing a puzzle." A discussion about what math is ensues. Maybe Nancy is doing math, the kind of math that's about shapes and curves and angles. No, math is paper and pencil; it's calculating. No, that's arithmetic; but math is more than that. Nancy may be doing the kind of math that's called geometry. This brief dialogue on the nature of mathematics concludes with agreement that Nancy needs harder puzzles.

At this point I say that I know a trick for multiplying by 9. Carol and David are interested. I write out 9 x 1, 9 x 2, etc., and ask if they can find the trick. "There's a pattern," I say. I have to help them a bit before David and Carol see that the last integers of the product are in descending order from 9 to 0 (9, 18, 27 ...). Carol is impressed but asks me how I *use* that. She just "knows" that 9 x 5 = 45; don't I? David excitedly interrupts to say that the first numbers go from 0 to 9! We look and then discover yet another pattern—each product adds up to 9 (18 = 1 + 8; 27 = 2 + 7; etc.). There is a bit of wonder and satisfaction on David's face. We ask each other why this happens and what it means, and joke that we have no idea if any of it is helpful in learning to multiply. We ask each other "How much is 9 x _?" and use the patterns to come up with the answers together. David, in particular, verbalizes the patterns.

Carol then tells us she knows a trick for multiplying by 11, that 11's were always hard for her until she learned this trick. David says that 11's are easy. Carol agrees that up to 11 x 9 they are, but when there are two numbers (i.e., double digit multiplication, for example, 11 x 14) it is hard and her trick makes it easy. She writes out 11 x 1, 11 x 2, up to 11 x 19 and challenges us to find the pattern. David quickly discovers that both columns of the product are in ascending order (11 x 1 = 11; 11 x 2 = 22; etc.). But what happens after 11 x 9 when the answer is over a hundred? Carol asks. The pattern continues for the tens and ones columns, but not the hundreds column. Carol tells us there's another pattern in multiplying 11's, and 11 x 11, 11 x 12, 11 x 13 reveal it. Can we see it? David and I are equally excited to learn/realize/discover "the trick"—you place the integer in the tens column of the multiplier in the hundreds column of the product, the integer in the ones column of the multiplier in the ones column of the product, and add the integers of the multiplier to get the number in the tens column of the product (in 11 x 12 = 132, 1 + 2 = 3, in 11 x 13 = 143, 1 + 3 = 4, etc.). But what about 11 x 19 = 209? Carol thinks maybe the pattern no longer holds—where did 209 come from? David shows us that it still works: 1 + 9 = 10, so 1 - 9 has to become 209! We create operations through 11 x 29 using our new discovery. The next day, David's mother reports that David said to her, "Hey Mom, I'm learning some math." (Holzman, 1995a, pp. 205–206)

The major point of this example is that it is essential to create discourse or "babble"—in this case, to "do math talk"—as part of the process of creating a developmental environment (a ZPD). If adults attempted to teach children to speak the way we typically attempt to teach children mathematics, the results would be not only ludicrous but a failure. Meaning-making is the developmental activity that must occur for learning to lead development; this is as true for learning to multiply as it is for learning to speak. In our culture, children are deprived fairly early in their lives of opportunities to make meaning or babble in mathematics (to perform as mathematicians). Formulaic ways of speaking and concern with correctness ("the right answer") come to dominate the discourse that occurs, stifling the kind of language play that, it would appear, is critical to learning a mathematical concept. On what basis do we assume that a mathematical concept or operation can be taught directly, that is, without the learners and teachers creating discourse? Just as meaning-making is a necessary precondition for learning to speak a language, making mathematical meaning is necessary for learning mathematics. Neither David nor the group as a whole knows how to do math talk very well; together they begin to make mathematical meaning together.

We turn now to a second, very different, example of creating a developmental environment, recounted by a staff member.

The students and learning directors were having lunch. Charles, a new student just beginning his third week at the school, begins to taunt Alice for being stupid. Both are 8 years old, he had just discovered. Charles had been in a gifted program in a public school and prided himself on being very smart. He was constantly getting into fights with other children, was identified as a problem student, and was routinely sent home from school. For these reasons, his mother decided to place him in the Barbara Taylor School; she thought he needed a more therapeutic environment where he would be supported to grow emotionally and socially.

When Charles loudly and incredulously proclaimed, "You don't know how to spell 'cat'! I don't believe you're in third grade!" learning director Len said to the group, "I need some help. Charles is playing the Competitive Game and it's turning into the Nasty Game." When I came over, Charles continuing to "marvel" at the fact that Alice could not spell 'cat.' He kept asking, "Why can't she spell 'cat'?" Alice was sinking lower in her seat, her head bowed. Len and some of the students attempted to change what was going on. They asked Charles why it mattered so much to him, why he was being nasty, and if he wanted to do something about it. A 12-year-old boy said matter of factly, "No one taught her to spell; that's why she can't." I told Charles I thought his question was a good one and that I had another good one—"How come he *could* spell 'cat'?" Charles said, "My mother taught me." Several of us pursued this: "How did she do it?" Charles said that his mother told him to watch the game shows on TV and he did; that's how he learned to spell.

During these conversational exchanges, Alice's brother Kevin whispered to her, "C-A-T" and she began to say repeatedly, "Cat—C-A-T." Charles shouted at Kevin, "Don't tell her! That's cheating." One of the students excitedly said, "She's learning it right now!" We asked Alice if she wanted to learn how to spell; she said she did. We asked Charles and the others if they thought Alice might be able to learn by watching game shows; they said yes. For the next 10 minutes an animated discussion took place on how to organize game show-spelling performances both at the school and for Alice at home. By the time lunch was over, it was decided that Charles and Len would be the co-producers and directors of the performances and four students had signed up to be the writers. Over the course of the next several days, the game show-spelling performance became an integrated activity of the school. On one day, Charles spent over an hour making a schedule of all the shows he thought Alice should watch. The writers spent time putting together flash cards to be used on the game show. Different students would come along and add a word or two throughout the course of the day.

Will Alice learn to spell? We do not know. And, in an important way, we do not particularly care. Our primary concern is that she (and others) learn that spelling is learnable! For learning that you are a learner is an essential component of developmental learning. It is generally accepted that a component of learning anything is learning how to learn, but learning how to learn is not the whole (developmental) story. Central to the Barbara Taylor School approach is the recognition that in learning something young children are learning not just two things but three: the particular thing learned; how to learn; and *that they are learners/that learning is something human beings do* (Holzman & Newman, 1987). It is this third "kind" of learning that acquisitional, knowledge-based learning leaves out. Without it, learning is separated from and often replaces development. The relational activity at the lunch table just described is, to my way of thinking, the process of creating a ZPD that makes it possible (but, of course, not inevitable) for developmental learning to occur, in part through the reintroduction—as a form of life—of this element of learning *as activity*.

This vignette is meant to illustrate some of the characteristics of developmental learning as a nonepistemological, therapeutic modality. The group activity was improvisational. The process of coming up with the idea for a collective game show-spelling performance was a reshaping of some of the elements in the existing environment to create something new—possibly learning. Charles' nastiness was not related to as either his problem or the adults' problem, but as something the group needed to deal with (a task raised by history in the course of our living together). We did not try to stop him from making fun of Alice (which would, in all likelihood, merely have stopped him temporarily). Instead, we tried (paraphrasing Wittgenstein) to draw his and everyone's attention to something else.

Taking his question seriously, we worked to reshape what he was giving—competitiveness and abuse (and curiosity, I think)—into something potentially developmental for the school as a whole. We created, among other things, a new language-game (we could call it the Curiosity Game or the How Do You Learn To Spell Game). Asking him how come he could spell and how he learned to do so was, as I see it, a bit of practical philosophizing. It reshaped the focus of the conversation from knowing to learning, from product to process, from fixed mental states and identities to relational possibilities. Perhaps in involving them in the beginnings of a new way of speaking, it freed Charles, Alice, and others from the one way of seeing things that the typical ways we use language tend to create. And, for the moment, no one was playing the Nasty Game.

Creating this environment engaged the students in a performance of creating their own learning–leading–development. Spelling is one of the infinite performances of which human beings are capable. Alice can perform as a speller (and create who she is by being who she is not). Charles can relate to her as a speller rather than as "a dummy." These new possibilities come into being simultaneously with the making of new meanings, through our language activity.

KNOWING DOES NOT ALWAYS EQUAL GROWTH

The Barbara Taylor School is an attempt to develop an educational practice that goes beyond challenging modernism's commitment to objective knowledge and dualistically divided objective and subjective worlds. Unlike many poststructuralists, social constructionists, and feminist epistemologists, our goal is not to recognize other "ways of knowing" nor to substitute a new, more relational, more constructionist form of knowing for the traditional one. Unlike the cognitively oriented Vygotskians, we do not view our task as supporting "socially situated and distributed knowledge" nor creating "communities of learners." These valuable educational and psychological reforms, in our view, do not get at the root of the educational crisis: knowing has become an impediment to developmental activity.

Our task is to help children develop, that is, *to create new ways of being.* We have constructed an approach that is postepistemological, by which I mean a practice that rejects the modernist belief that knowing (of any sort) is the path to a better life and/or a better world (or progress or growth). Developmental learning is an attempt to give up the alienated activity/institution of knowing in favor of the noncognitive, nondualistic activity of performing. No doubt, all that is known will continue to co-exist even as children perform their development. No doubt, they will come to know many things, even as they perform increasingly as nonknowers. Guided by the emergent continuousness of our activity rather than by the need to know what we are doing or what its purpose or outcome will be, we have tried to create a school where children come—not in order to know—but in order to grow.[2]

---

[2]I would like to thank Routledge for allowing me to reproduce passages on pp. 107–108, 114–115, and 130–131, which are similar to those found in chapter 5 of *The End of Knowing*.

Chapter 8

Not a Conclusion

◆ ◆ ◆

To varying degrees and in different ways, the Golden Key project, the Sudbury Valley School, and the Barbara Taylor School challenge the glorification of knowledge production and acquisition that is the officially sanctioned *raison d'etre* of schools and, as I have argued, a major source of their failure. They reject some of the more obvious structures that support the knowing paradigm—curriculum and subjects, grades and testing, and age sorting and homogeneous groups—in favor of (again, to varying degrees and in different ways) the activity of environment-building. As I see it, the developmental potential of these educational projects derives from the extent to which they are engaged in the process of creating nonepistemological environments.

That these schools have been able to go farther in their positive critique of traditional models than most, if not all, public schools raises the issue of the *practicality* of their radicalness. On the one hand, they raise critically important questions about the direction of contemporary educational reform. If one is very open to the spirit of their methodological challenge, then I believe these alternatives can serve as a rich source of inspiration. For their key characteristics—performance and democracy—are far from foreign terms when it comes to discussions of educational reform. These topics are, in fact, relatively well known to educators and educational researchers, and they are increasingly being raised in recognition of the critical historical moment that is, by so many accounts, the end of the modern era.

For example, the call to transform schools into democratic institutions has been voiced in the context of the ethical–practical question of whether or not we will be able to transform how human beings relate to each other before it is too late. This goes beyond the modernist concern (that Dewey, for example, so forcefully expressed) to prepare children for active and reasoned citizenship in a democracy. What is new is the subjective dimension, a recognition that reason and rationality will not do and, further, that the cognitive–affective split institutionalized in Western culture needs to be abandoned. Thus, for some educators the need for democratic education is related to the crisis in subjectivity, in particular, the pervasive sense of hopelessness and disconnection that millions of people (not only in the United States) feel and the uncaring and often violent actions that accompany such subjectivity.

Noddings, for example, insisted "that our aim should be to encourage the growth of competent, caring, loving, and lovable persons" (1996); Carlson argued that we must recapture a "lost sense of hope and possibility" (1996); and Clinchy called for an educational model based on "care, concern, and connection" (1996). The hope is that active participation in creating learning communities that are democratic and inclusive will produce the desired changes in ways of relating. It is the developmental (the subjective and activistic) aspects of democracy that I find promising in this line of inquiry. That is, to invoke Vygotsky's tool-and-result methodology once again, it is the building of environments in which democratic process can emerge, rather than the imposing of democratic structures on existing learning environments, that is growthful.

Similarly, it is the reinitiation of possibility that I find significant in the intellectual/disciplinary approach known as performance studies, a methodology that holds much promise to educational researchers and classroom teachers alike. Seeing the teaching and learning process as performance potentially allows one to see and create new things, including performatory pedagogy.

The benefits of a performative approach to education have been argued by Pineau (1994). In "Teaching is Performance: Reconceptualizing a Problematic Metaphor," she drew connections between critical pedagogy and performance studies, concluding that a performance-centered approach is "inherently, and exhilaratingly, countercultural at both the pedagogical and theoretical levels" (p. 21). Pineau's article touched on many of the issues I have discussed in relation to the problems of the epistemological paradigm that dominates education and stifles developmental activity (what Vygotsky called "the only good learning"—learning that leads development). Here are some of the benefits she attributes to a performance approach to education:

> The disciplinary dictum that performance enables a "sense of the other" is grounded in the commitment to engage multiple—often contradictory—modes of experience in an intimate, nonjudgemental, and dialogic manner. Certainly the performance method itself, with its commitment to participatory, kinesthetic learning, dismantles the rational bias of traditional instruction. Performance studies is also committed to blurring the arbitrary boundaries between social and educational contexts.... Likewise, the collaborative nature of performance blurs the boundaries between teachers and students. Workshops and rehearsals bring the instructor into the student's space, where they must

work together as partners in the learning experience … In effect, to be a scholar or
teacher of performance means welcoming students to join us in that uncertain,
magical space of personal and communal transformation. (Pineau, 1994, p. 21)

Notice that for Pineau it is performance that subverts knowing and its
authoritarianism. This is, in my opinion, a troublesome presumption that is
insufficiently dialectical and activistic, and inattentive to environment. The
position I have been putting forth (presented in depth in the discussion of
the developing development community in chapters 1 and 4) suggests that
it is the *creating of a nonepistemological environment* that is so vital. "Doing"
performance in a traditionally organized educational environment (one in
which knowing dominates) will not, in my opinion, subvert knowing. More
than likely it will make knowing more fun and perhaps easier, but performance in itself presents little challenge to knowing and its companions truth
and objectivity. It is, rather, the activity of creating nonepistemological
environments that makes *developmental performance* possible.

Thus, Pineau's ideas, although confined to the topic of *teaching* as
performance, are both consistent and inconsistent with the analysis and
illustrations I have presented on learning as performance and performance
as developmental (revolutionary) activity. So, too, are the various studies
exploring the important role of drama, theater, and culture in the classroom
(see, e.g., Heath, 1993). Bringing the new conceptualization of development—as the tool-and-result building of an environment that supports
developmental activity *and* the developmental activity it supports—into
these discussions would, I think, create an enriched dialogue.

We began with the question, "Is there anything teachers can do in
nondevelopmental environments?" Our explorations—into the philosophical structure of education, the deconstruction of psychology's conceptualization of learning and development, their reconstruction into
developmental learning and performatory activity via a revolutionary reading of Vygotsky and an activity–theoretic reading of Wittgenstein, and the
presentation of three radical educational alternatives and their developmental potential—are, I hope, not construed as *an answer* to this question.

I say this because if there is anything of value in what I have presented it
is, in my opinion, to be found in the questioning activity itself—the
meandering through philosophical territory (and jargon), psychology's history, postmodernism's social constructionism and performance studies,
Marxist activity theory, and the lives of a small number of children and
adults in Moscow, Massachusetts, and New York City who came together
for a time and created some things they believed to be of value. No doubt,
hundreds of questions were generated as you read (observed, participated
in this questioning activity). My hope is that among your questions are not
only ones like "Is this true?" "Will that work?" and "Do I agree?" but also
"Can I do that?"

References

Apple, M.W. (1979). *Ideology and curriculum*. London: Routledge & Kegan Paul.
Ariès, P. (1962). *Centuries of childhood: A social history of family life*. New York: Vintage Books.
Baker, G. P. (1992). Some remarks on "language" and "grammar." *Grazer Philosophische Studien, 42,* 107–131.
Bakhtin, M. M. (1981). *The dialogic imagination: Four essays by M. M. Bakhtin*. Austin: University of Texas Press.
Bakhurst, D. (1991). *Consciousness and revolution in Soviet philosophy*. Cambridge: Cambridge University Press.
Bakhurst, D. (1995). Wittgenstein and social being. In D. Bakhurst & C. Sypnowich (Eds.), *The social self* (pp. 30–46). London: Sage.
Baritz, L. (1960). *The servants of power: A history of the use of social science in American industry*. Westport, CT: Greenwood.
Best, S., & Kellner, D. (1991). *Postmodern theory: Critical interrogations*. New York: Guilford.
Blanck, G. (1990). Vygotsky: The man and his cause. In L. Moll (Ed.), *Vygotsky and education* (pp. 31–58). Cambridge: Cambridge University Press.
Bloom, L. (1970). *Language development: Form and function in emerging grammars*. Cambridge, MA: MIT Press.
Bloom, L. (1973). *One word at a time: The use of single-word utterances*. The Hague, Netherlands: Mouton.
Bloom, L. (1991). *Language development from two to three*. Cambridge: Cambridge University Press.
Bloom, L., Hood, L., & Lightbown, P. (1974). Imitation in language development: If, when and why. *Cognitive Psychology, 6,* 380–420. Reprinted in L. Bloom (1991), *Language development from two to three* (pp. 399–433). Cambridge: Cambridge University Press.
Bowles, S., & Gintis, H. (1976). *Schooling in capitalist America*. New York: Basic Books.
Bradley, B. S., & Kessen, W. (Eds.), (1993). Special issue: The future of development theory. *Theory & Psychology, 3*(4), 403–558.
Broughton, J. M. (Ed.), (1987). *Critical theories of psychological development*. New York: Plenum.

Brown, A. L. (1994). The advancement of learning. *Educational Researcher, 23*(8), 4–12.

Bruner, J. S. (1996, September). *Celebrating divergence: Piaget and Vygotsky.* Keynote address presented at the "Growing Mind" conference and "Vygotsky–Piaget" conference, Geneva, Switzerland.

Bruner, J. S., Jolly, A., & Sylva, K. (Eds.). (1976). *Play: Its role in development and evolution.* New York: Basic Books.

Bulhan, H. A. (1985). *Frantz Fanon and the psychology of oppression.* New York: Plenum.

Burman, E. (Ed.). (1990). *Feminists and psychological practice.* London: Sage.

Burman, E. (1994). *Deconstructing developmental psychology.* London: Routledge.

Carlson, D. (1996). *Making progress: Education and culture in new times.* New York: Teachers College Press.

Chaiklin, S., & Lave, J. (Eds.). (1993). *Understanding practice: Perspectives on activity and context.* Cambridge: Cambridge University Press.

Chapman, M., & Dixon, R. A. (Eds.). (1987). *Meaning and the growth of understanding: Wittgenstein's significance for developmental psychology.* Berlin: Springer.

Chomsky, N. (1959). A review of B. F. Skinner's *Verbal Behavior. Language, 35*(1), 26–58.

Clinchy, E. (1996). *Transforming public education: A new course for America's future.* New York: Teachers College Press.

Cole, M. (1985). The zone of proximal development: When culture and cognition create each other. In J. V. Wertsch (Ed.), *Culture, communication and cognition: Vygotskian perspectives* (pp. 146–161). Cambridge: Cambridge University Press.

Cole, M. (1995). Culture and cognitive development: From cross-cultural research to creating systems of cultural mediation. *Culture and Psychology, 1,* 25–54.

Cole, M., & Engestrom, Y. (1993). A cultural–historical approach to distributed cognition. In G. Salomon (Ed.), *Distributed cognitions: Psychological and educational considerations.* Cambridge: Cambridge University Press.

Cole, M., Hood, L., & McDermott, R. P. (1978). *Ecological niche-picking: Ecological validity as an axiom of experimental cognitive psychology* (Monograph). New York: Rockefeller University, Laboratory of Comparative Human Cognition. [Reprinted in *Practice, 4*(1), 117–129].

Coles, G. (1987). *The learning mystique: A critical look at learning disabilities.* New York: Pantheon.

Cushman, P. (1991). Ideology obscured: Political uses of the self in Daniel Stern's infant. *American Psychologist, 46,* 206–219.

Cushman, P. (1995). *Constructing the self, constructing America: A cultural history of psychotherapy.* Reading, MA: Addison-Wesley.

Daniels, H. (Ed.). (1993). *Charting the agenda: Educational activity after Vygotsky.* London: Routledge.

Daniels, H. (Ed.). (1996). *An introduction to Vygotsky.* London: Routledge.

Danziger, K. (1994). *Constructing the subject: Historical origins of psychological research.* Cambridge: Cambridge University Press.

Davydov, V. V. (1988). Problems of developmental teaching: the experience of theoretical and experimental psychological research. *Soviet Education, XXX*(8), 3–87.

Davydov, V. V. (1995). The influence of L. S. Vygotsky on education theory, research, and practice. *Educational Researcher, 24*(3), 12–21.

Dawes, R. M. (1994). *House of cards: Psychology and psychotherapy built on myth.* New York: The Free Press.

Dixon-Krauss, L. (Ed.). (1996). *Vygotsky in the classroom: Mediated literacy instruction and assessment.* White Plains, NY: Longman.

Elkind, D. (1991). Developmentally appropriate practice: A case study of educational inertia. In S. L. Kagen (Ed.), *The care and education of America's young children: Obstacles and opportunities. Nineteenth yearbook of the National Society for the Study of Education* (pp. 1–16). Chicago: University of Chicago Press.

Elkonin, D., & Davydov, V. V. (Eds.), (1966). *Learning possibilities at different ages.* Moscow: Prosvescenie.

Fine, M. (1991). *Framing dropouts: Notes on the politics of an urban public high school.* Albany: State University of New York Press.

Fine, M. (Ed.). (1994). *Charting urban school reform: Reflections on public high schools in the midst of change.* New York: Teachers College Press.

Finlan, T. G. (1994). *Learning disability: The imaginary disease.* Westport, CT: Bergin & Garvey.

Freire, P. (1972). *Pedagogy of the oppressed.* New York: Herder & Herder.

Friedman, D. (1990). The Soviet Union in the 1920s: An historical laboratory. *Practice, The Magazine of Psychology and Political Economy, 7,* 5–9.

Gergen, K. J. (1982). *Toward transformation in social knowledge.* London: Sage.

Gergen, K. J. (1994). *Realities and relationships: Soundings in social construction.* Cambridge, MA: Harvard University Press.

Gergen, K. J. (1995, April). *Social construction and the transformation of identity politics.* Paper presented at the New School for Social Research, New York City.

Gergen, K. J., & Kaye, J. (1993). Beyond narrative in the negotiation of therapeutic meaning. In S. McNamee & K. J. Gergen (Eds.), *Therapy as social construction* (pp. 166–187). London: Sage.

Gilligan, C. (1982). *In a different voice: Psychological theory and women's development.* Cambridge, MA: Harvard University Press.

Giroux, H. (1983). *Theory and resistance: A pedagogy for the opposition.* S. Hadley, MA: Bergin & Garvey.

Giroux, H. (1993). *Border crossings: Cultural workers and the politics of education.* New York: Routledge.

Gould, S. J. (1996). *Full house: The spread of excellence from Plato to Darwin.* New York: Harmony Books.

Greenberg, D. (1973). *"Announcing a new school … ": A personal account of the beginnings of The Sudbury Valley School.* Framingham, MA: Sudbury Valley School Press.

Greenberg, D. (1987). *The Sudbury Valley School experience.* Framingham, MA: Sudbury Valley School Press.

Greenberg, D. (1992). *A new look at schools.* Framingham, MA: Sudbury Valley School Press.

Greenberg, D., & Sadofsky, M. (1992). *Legacy of trust: Life after the Sudbury Valley School Experience.* Framingham, MA: Sudbury Valley School Press.

Greer, C. (1972). *The great school legend: A revisionist interpretation of American public education.* New York: Basic Books.

Gruber, H. E., & Voneche, J. J. (1977). *The essential Piaget.* New York: Basic Books.

Heath, S. B. (1993). Inner city life through drama: Imagining the language classroom. *TESOL Quarterly, 27*(2), 177–192.

Hedegaard, M., Hakkarainen, P., & Engestrom, Y. (1984). *Learning and teaching on a scientific basis: Methodological and epistemological aspects of the activity theory of learning and teaching.* Aarhus, Denmark: Aarhus Universited Psykologisk Institut.

Henriques, J., Holloway, W., Urwin, C., Venn, C., & Walkerdine, V. (Eds.). (1984). *Changing the subject: Psychology, social regulation and subjectivity.* London: Methuen.

Hiebert, J., Carpenter, T. P., Fennema, E., Fuson, K., Human, P., Murray, H., Olivier, A., & Wearne, D. (1996). Problem solving as a basis for reform in curriculum and instruction: The case of mathematics. *Educational Researcher, 25*(4), 12–21.

Holmes, S. A. (1996, June 20). Income disparity between poorest and richest rises. *The New York Times*, pp. A1, A18.

Holzman, L. (1982). Pragmatism and dialectical materialism in language development. In K. E. Nelson (Ed.), *Children's language* (pp. 345–367). Hillsdale, NJ: Lawrence Erlbaum Associates. Reprinted in H. Daniels, Ed., (1996) *Introduction to Vygotsky*, (pp. 75–98). London: Routledge.

Holzman, L. (1993). Notes from the laboratory: A work-in-progress report from the Barbara Taylor School. *Practice, the Magazine of Psychology and Political Economy, 9*(1), 25–37.

Holzman, L. (1995a). Creating developmental learning environments: A Vygotskian practice. *School Psychology International, 16*, 199–212.

Holzman, L. (1995b). Creating the zone: Reflections on the International Conference on L. S. Vygotsky and the Contemporary Human Sciences. *School Psychology International, 16*(2), 213–216.

Holzman, L. (1995c). "Wrong," said Fred. A response to Parker. *Changes: An International Journal of Psychology and Psychotherapy, 13*(1), 23–26.

Holzman, L. (1996). Newman's practice of method completes Vygotsky. In I. Parker & R. Spears (Eds.), *Psychology and society: Radical theory and practice* (pp. 128–138). London: Pluto.

Holzman, L., & Newman, F. (1979). *The practice of method: An introduction to the foundations of social therapy*. New York: New York Institute for Social Therapy & Research.

Holzman, L., & Newman, F. (1987). Language and thought about history. In M. Hickmann (Ed.), *Social and functional approaches to language and thought*, (pp. 109–121). London: Academic Press.

Holzman, L., & Polk, H. (Eds.). (1988). *History is the cure: A social therapy reader.* New York: Practice Press.

Hood, L., McDermott, R. P., & Cole, M. (1980). "Let's try to make it a good day"—Some not so simple ways. *Discourse Processes, 3*, 155–168.

hooks, b. (1994). *Teaching to transgress: Education as the practice of freedom.* London: Routledge.

Horgan, J. (1996). *The end of science: Facing the limits of knowledge in the twilight of the scientific age.* Reading, MA: Addison-Wesley.

Ingleby, D. (Ed.). (1980). *Critical psychiatry: The politics of mental health.* New York: Pantheon.

Janik, A., & Toulmin, S. (1973). *Wittgenstein's Vienna.* New York: Simon & Schuster.

John-Steiner, V., Panofsky, C., & Smith, L. (Eds.). (1994). *Sociocultural approaches to language and literacy: An interactionist perspective.* Cambridge: Cambridge University Press.

Joravsky, D. (1989). *Russian psychology: A critical history.* Oxford, England: Blackwell.

Jost, J. (1995). Toward a Wittgensteinian social psychology of human development. *Theory & Psychology, 5*(1), 5–25.

Kamin, L. J. (1974). *The science and politics of I.Q.* Potomac, MD: Lawrence Erlbaum Associates.

Kaye, K. (1982). *The mental and social life of babies.* Chicago: University of Chicago Press.

Kohlberg, L., & Mayer, R. (1972). Development as the aim of education. *Harvard Educational Review, 42*(4), 449–496.

Kozulin, A. (1990). *Vygotsky's psychology: A biography of ideas.* Cambridge, MA: Harvard University Press.

Kvale, S. (Ed.). (1992). *Psychology and postmodernism.* London: Sage.

LaCerva, C. (1992). Talking about talking about sex: The organization of possibilities. In J. T. Sears (Ed.), *Sexuality and the curriculum: The politics and practice of sexuality education* (pp. 124–138). New York: Teachers College Press.

Laing, R. D. (1959). *The divided self.* London: Tavistock.

Lasch, C. (1976). The family as a haven in a heartless world. *Salamagundi, 35.*

Lave, J., & Wenger, E. (1991). *Situated learning: Legitimate peripheral participation.* Cambridge: Cambridge University Press.

Lawler, J. (1978). *IQ, heritability and racism.* New York: International Publishers.

Levitin, K. (1982). *One is not born a personality: Profiles of Soviet education psychologists.* Moscow: Progress Publishers.

Lyotard, J-F. (1984). *The postmodern condition: A report on knowledge.* Minneapolis: University of Minnesota Press.

Marx, K. (1973). Theses on Feuerbach. In K. Marx & F. Engels (Eds.), *The German ideology* (pp. 121–123). New York: International Publishers.

Marx, K., & Engels, F. (1973). *The German ideology.* New York: International Publishers.

McDermott, R. P., & Hood, L. (1982). Institutionalized psychology and the ethnography of schooling. In P. Gilmore & A. A. Glatthorn (Eds.), *Children in and out of school: Ethnography and education* (pp. 232–249). Washington, DC: Center for Applied Linguistics.

McLaren, P. (1989). *Life in schools.* New York: Longman.

McLaren, P. (1995). *Critical pedagogy and predatory culture: Opposition politics in a postmodern era.* New York: Routledge.

McNamee, S., & Gergen, K. J. (Eds.). (1993). *Therapy as social construction.* London: Sage.

Miller, P. H. (1993). *Theories of developmental psychology.* New York: Freeman.

Miller, R. (1992). *What are schools for? Holistic education in American culture.* Brandon, VT: Holistic Education Press.

Mintz, J. (Ed.). (1995). *The almanac of education choices: Private and public learning alternatives and homeschooling.* New York: Macmillan.

Moll, L. C. (Ed.). (1990). *Vygotsky and education: Instructional implications and applications of sociocultural psychology.* Cambridge: Cambridge University Press.

Monk, R. (1990). *Ludwig Wittgenstein: The duty of genius.* New York: Penguin.

Morss, J. (1990). *The biologising of childhood: Developmental psychology and the Darwinian myth.* East Sussex: Lawrence Erlbaum Associates, Ltd.

Morss, J. (1992). Making waves: Deconstruction and developmental psychology. *Theory & Psychology, 2*(4), 445–65.

Morss, J. (1993). Spirited away: A consideration of the anti-developmental Zeitgeist. *Practice, The Magazine of Psychology and Political Economy, 9*(2), 22–28.

Morss, J. (1995). *Growing critical: Alternatives to developmental psychology.* London: Routledge.

Murray, B. (1996). Home schools: How do they affect children? *APA Monitor, 27,* pp. 1, 43.

Napoli, D. S. (1981). *Architects of adjustment: The history of the psychological profession in the United States.* Port Washington, NY: Kennikat Press.

The National Education Goals Report (1995). *Building a nation of learners.* Washington, DC: National Education Goals Panel.

Newman, D., Griffin, P., & Cole, M. (1989). *The construction zone: Working for cognitive change in school.* Cambridge: Cambridge University Press.

Newman, F. (1991a). Community as a heart in a havenless world. In F. Newman (Ed.), *The myth of psychology* (pp. 140–157). New York: Castillo International.

Newman, F. (1991b). *The myth of psychology.* New York: Castillo International.

Newman, F. (1994). *Let's develop! A guide to continuous personal growth.* New York: Castillo International.

Newman, F. (1996). *Performance of a lifetime: A practical–philosophical guide to the joyous life.* New York: Castillo International.

Newman, F., & Holzman, L. (1993). *Lev Vygotsky: Revolutionary scientist.* London: Routledge.

Newman, F., & Holzman, L. (1996). *Unscientific psychology: A cultural–performatory approach to understanding human life.* Westport, CT: Praeger.

Newman, F., & Holzman, L. (1997). *The end of knowing: A new developmental way of learning.* London: Routledge.

Noddings, N. (1996). *The challenge to care in school.* New York: Teachers College Press.

Perkinson, H. J. (1993). *Teachers without goals, students without purposes.* New York: McGraw-Hill.

Perlman, L. J. (1992). *School's out: A radical new formula for the revitalization of America's educational system.* New York: Avon.

Peterman, J. F. (1992). *Philosophy as therapy: An interpretation and defense of Wittgenstein's later philosophical project.* Albany: State University of New York Press.

Peters, M. (Ed.). (1995). *Education and the postmodern condition.* Westport, CT: Bergin & Garvey.

Piaget, J. (1955). *The language and thought of the child.* London: Kegan Paul.

Pineau, E. L. (1994). Teaching is performance: Reconceptualizing a problematic metaphor. *American Educational Research Journal, 31*(1), 3–25.

Polkinghorne, D. (1983). *Methodology for the human sciences: Systems of inquiry.* Albany: State University of New York Press.

Ratner, C. (1991). *Vygotsky's sociohistorical psychology and its contemporary applications.* New York: Plenum.

Readings, B. (1991). *Introducing Lyotard: Art and politics.* London: Routledge.

Richardson, L. (1995, October 17). Special education loses money, but not students. *The New York Times,* pp. A1, B8.

Rivlin, L. G., & Wolfe, M. (1985). *Institutional settings in children's lives.* New York: Wiley.

Rogoff, B. (1990). *Apprenticeship in thinking: Cognitive development in social context.* New York: Oxford University Press.

Rogoff, B., & Lave, J. (Eds.). (1984). *Everyday cognition: Its development in social contexts.* Cambridge, MA: Harvard University Press.

Rothstein, S. W. (1994). *Schooling the poor: A social inquiry into the American educational experience.* Westport, CT: Bergin & Garvey.

Rust, F. O. (1993). *Changing teaching, changing schools: Bringing early childhood practice into public education.* New York: Teachers College Press.

Sadofsky, M., & Greenberg, D. (1994). *Kingdom of childhood: Growing up at Sudbury Valley School.* Framingham, MA: Sudbury Valley School Press.

Samelson, F. (1979). Putting psychology on the map: Ideology and intelligence testing. In A. R. Buss (Ed.), *Psychology in social context* (pp. 103–168). New York: Irvington.

Shotter, J. (1991). Wittgenstein and psychology: On our 'hook up'to reality. In A. Phillips-Griffiths (Ed.), Wittgenstein: Centenary essays (pp. 193–208). Cambridge: Cambridge University Press.

Shotter, J. (1993a). Conversational realities: Studies in social constructionism. London: Sage.

Shotter, J. (1993b). Cultural politics of everyday life: Social constructionism, rhetoric and knowing of the third kind. Toronto: University of Toronto Press.

Shotter, J. (1995). In conversation: Joint action, shared intentionality and ethics. Theory & Psychology, 5(1), 49–73.

Singer, E. (1993). Shared care for children. Theory & Psychology, 3(4), 427–449.

Skinner, B. F. (1959). Verbal behavior. New York: Appleton-Century-Crofts.

Slattery, P. (1995). Curriculum development in the postmodern era. New York: Garland.

Smeyers, P., & Marshall, J. D. (Eds.). (1995). Philosophy and education: Accepting Wittgenstein's challenge. Dordrecht, Holland: Kluwer.

Steward, E. P. (1995). Beginning writers in the zone of proximal development. Hillsdale, NJ: Lawrence Erlbaum Associates.

Strickland, G., & Holzman, L. (1989). Developing poor and minority children as leaders with the Barbara Taylor School Educational Model. Journal of Negro Education, 58(3), 383–398.

Sudbury Valley School Press. (1996). Evaluations of the Sudbury Valley School: How educators see us. The SVS Press Newsletter, 26(1), 16–24.

Sutton-Smith, B. (1976). The psychology of play. Salem, NH: Ayer.

Szasz, T. (1961). The myth of mental illness: Foundations of a theory of personal conduct. New York: Harper & Row.

Szasz, T. (1996). The meaning of mind: Language, morality and neuroscience. Westport, CT: Praeger.

Taylor, D. (1991). Learning denied. Portsmouth, NH: Heinemann.

Tharp, R. G., & Gallimore, R. (1988). Rousing minds to life: Teaching, learning and schooling in social context. Cambridge: Cambridge University Press.

Timpanero, S. (1985). The Freudian slip: Psychoanalysis and textual criticism. London: Verso.

Torrey, E. F. (1992). Freudian fraud. New York: HarperCollins.

Trevarthan, C., & Hubley, P. (1978). Secondary intersubjectivity: Confidence, confiding and acts of meaning in the first year. In A. Lock (Ed.), Action, gesture and symbol: The emergence of language (pp. 183–229). New York: Academic Press.

van der Merwe, W. L., & Voestermans, P. P. (1995). Wittgenstein's legacy and the challenge to psychology. Theory & Psychology, 5(1) , 27–48.van der Veer, R., & Valsiner, J. (1991). Understanding Vygotsky: A quest for synthesis. Oxford, England: Blackwell.

van der Veer, R., & Valsiner, J. (Eds.). (1994). The Vygotsky reader. Oxford, England: Blackwell.

Vygodskaya, G. (1996). Remembering Lev Vygotsky. In L. Fulani (Ed.), Women who won't sell out (pp. 158–163). New York: Castillo International.

Vygotsky, L. S. (1978). Mind in society. Cambridge, MA: Harvard University Press.

Vygotsky, L. S. (1982). The historical meaning of the crisis in psychology. In A. R. Luria & M. G. Iaroshevski (Eds.), L. S. Vygotsky: Collected Works, Vol. 1. Moscow: Pedagogika. [In Russian.]

Vygotsky, L. S. (1987). The collected works of L. S. Vygotsky. Vol. 1. New York: Plenum.

Vygotsky, L. S. (1993). The collected works of L. S. Vygotsky. Vol. 2. New York: Plenum.

Vygotsky, L. S. (1994). The problem of the environment. In R. van der Veer & J. Valsiner (Eds.), *The Vygotsky reader* (pp. 338–354). Oxford, England: Blackwell

Walkerdine, V. (1984). Developmental psychology and the child-centered pedagogy: The insertion of Piaget into early education. In J. Henriques, W. Holloway, C. Urwin, C. Venn & V. Walkerdine (Eds.), *Changing the subject: Psychology, social regulation and subjectivity* (pp. 153–202). London: Methuen.

Walkerdine, V. (1988). *The mastery of reason.* London: Routledge.

Watt, J. (1994). *Ideology, objectivity and education.* New York: Teachers College Press.

Wertsch, J. V. (Ed.). (1985a). *Culture, communication and cognition: Vygotskian perspectives.* Cambridge: Cambridge University Press.

Wertsch, J. V. (1985b). *Vygotsky and the social formation of mind.* Cambridge, MA: Harvard University Press.

Wertsch, J. V. (1991). *Voices of the mind. A sociocultural approach to mediated action.* Cambridge, MA: Harvard University Press.

Wittgenstein, L. (1953). *Philosophical investigations.* Oxford, England: Blackwell.

Wittgenstein, L. (1961). *Tractatus logico-philosophicus.* London: Routledge.

Wittgenstein, L. (1965). *The blue and brown books.* New York: Harper Torchbooks.

Wittgenstein, L. (1967). *Zettel.* Oxford, England: Blackwell.

Wittgenstein, L. (1980). *Remarks on the philosophy of psychology. Vol. I.* Oxford, England: Blackwell.

Wood, G. (1992). *Schools that work: America's most innovative public education programs.* New York: Plume.

Zelizer, V. A. (1985). *Pricing the priceless child: The changing value of children.* New York: Basic Books.

Author Index

♦ ♦ ♦

A

Apple, M. W., 41n, 130
Ariès, P., 21, 130

B

Baker, G. P., 67, 69, 130
Bakhtin, M. M., 32, 130
Bakhurst, D., 45, 47, 130
Baritz, L., 26, 130
Best, S., 6n, 130
Blanck, G., 54, 130
Bloom, L., 8, 62, 130
Bowles, S., 41, 130
Bradley, B., 2n, 130
Broughton, J. M., 2n, 130
Brown, A. L., 39, 131
Bruner, J. S., 109, 131
Bulhan, H. A., 2n, 34, 131
Burman, E., 2n, 21, 22, 28, 31, 34, 131
Burt, 46n

C

Carlson, D., 28, 131
Carpenter, T. P., 39, 133
Chaiklin, S., 43n, 131
Chapman, M., 67, 131
Chomsky, N., 27, 131

Clinchy, E., 128, 131
Cole, M., 41, 42, 43, 43n, 55n, 66, 131, 133, 135
Coles, G., 19, 131
Cushman, P., 24, 26, 34, 131

D

Daniels, H., 43n, 131
Danziger, K., 12, 26, 35, 36, 36n, 37, 131
Davydov, V. V., 72, 132
Dawes, R. M., 65, 131
Dixon, R. A., 67, 131
Dixon-Krauss, L., 43n, 131

E

Elkind, D., 39, 132
Elkonin, D., 72, 132
Engels, F., 11, 134
Engestrom, Y., 42, 43n, 131, 132

F

Fennema, E., 39, 133
Fine, M., 41, 132
Finlan, T. G., 19, 132
Freidman, D., 54, 132
Freire, P., 41, 132

Fuson, K., 39, 133

G

Galllimore, R., 43n, 136
Gergen, K. J., 6n, 12, 47, 48, 49, 65, 67, 132, 134
Gilligan, C., 2n, 34, 132
Gintis, H., 41, 130
Giroux, H., 41, 132
Gould, S. J., 34, 132
Greenberg, D., 94, 95, 96, 98, 99, 100, 102, 104, 105, 132, 135
Greer, C., 41, 132
Griffin, P., 42, 43, 135
Gruber, H. E., 28, 29, 132

H

Hakkarainen, P., 43n, 132
Heath, S. B., 129, 132
Hedegaard, M., 43n, 132
Henriques, J., 2n, 132
Hiebert, J., 39, 133
Holloway, W., 2n, 132
Holmes, S. A., 16, 133
Holzman, L., 11, 12, 13, 20n, 23, 26, 28, 37, 43, 47, 48, 49, 50, 52, 53, 54, 59, 60, 62, 65, 66, 68, 69, 71, 72, 73, 74, 76, 77, 78, 113, 117, 122, 123, 125, 133, 135, 136
Hood, L., 9, 41, 42, 55n, 62, 130, 131, 133, 134
hooks, b., 41n, 133
Horgan, J., 6, 133
Hubley, P., 32, 136
Human, P., 39, 133

I

Ingleby, D., 65, 133

J

Janik, A., 67n, 133
John-Steiner, V., 43n, 133
Jolly, A., 109, 131
Joravsky, D., 54, 133
Jost, J., 68, 133

K

Kamin, L. J., 36, 133
Kaye, J., 67, 132
Kaye, K., 32, 33, 34, 133
Kellner, D., 6n, 130
Kessen, W., 2n, 130
Kohlberg, L., 134
Kozulin, A., 43, 43n, 54, 134
Kravtsov, G., 85, 86, 88, 89, 91, 92
Kravtsova, E., 85, 86, 88, 89, 91, 92
Kuhn, T., 46n
Kvale, S., 6n, 47, 134

L

LaCerva, C., 113, 134
Laing, R. D., 64, 134
Lasch, C., 93, 134
Lave, J., 43n, 66, 72, 131, 134, 135
Lawler, J., 36, 134
Levitin, K., 23, 43n, 134
Lightbown, P., 62, 130
Lyotard, J-F., 6n, 134

M

Marshall, J. D., 101, 136
Marx, K., 11, 43, 64, 134
Mayer, R., 134
McDermott, R. P., 9, 41, 42, 55n, 131, 133, 134
McLaren, P., 41n, 134
McNamee, S., 65, 134
Miller, P. H., 134
Miller, R., 81, 134
Mintz, J., 81, 134
Moll, L. C., 43n, 134
Monk, R., 71, 134
Morss, J., 2n, 21, 22, 34, 43, 134
Murray, B., 7n, 134
Murray, H., 39, 133

N

Napoli, D. S., 26, 134
The National Education Goals Report, 18, 135
Newman, D., 12, 42, 43, 71, 76, 106, 135

Newman, F., 11, 12, 13, 20n, 23, 26, 28, 37, 42, 43, 47, 48, 49, 50, 52, 53, 54, 59, 60, 62, 65, 66, 68, 69, 71, 72, 73, 74, 76, 125, 133, 135
Noddings, N., 128, 135

O

Olivier, A., 39, 133

P

Panofsky, C., 43n, 133
Perkinson, H. J., 48, 135
Perlman, L. J., 19, 135
Peterman, J. F., 67, 135
Peters, M., 6n, 48, 135
Piaget, J., 29, 30, 135
Pineau, E. L., 128, 135
Polk, H., 76, 133
Polkinghorne, D., 12, 47, 135

R

Ratner, C., 43n, 135
Readings, B., 6n, 135
Richardson, L., 18, 135
Rivlin, L. G., 35, 135
Rogoff, B., 43n, 66, 72, 135
Rothstein, S. W., 16, 135
Rust. F. O., 40, 109, 109n, 135

S

Sadofsky, M., 94, 102, 104, 132, 135
Samelson, F., 36, 135
Shotter, J., 12, 47, 53, 66, 68, 69, 136
Singer, E., 34, 136
Skinner, B. F., 27, 136
Slattery, P., 48, 136
Smeyers, P., 101, 136
Smith, L., 43n, 133
Steward, E. P., 43, 136
Strickland, G., 113, 136

Sudbury Valley School Press, 95, 136
Sutton-Smith, B., 109, 136
Sylva, K., 109, 131
Szasz, T., 65, 136

T

Taylor, D., 19, 136
Tharp, R.G., 43n, 136
Timpanero, S., 65, 136
Torrey, E. F., 24, 26, 65, 136
Toulmin, S., 67n, 133
Trevarthan, C., 32, 136

U

Urwin, C., 2n, 132

V

Valsiner, J., 43n, 53, 53n, 54, 136
van der Merwe, W. L., 68, 69, 136
van der Veer, R., 43n, 53, 53n, 54, 136
Venn, C., 2n, 132
Voestermans, P. P., 68, 69, 136
Voneche, J. J., 28, 29, 132
Vygodskaya, G., 54, 136
Vygotsky, L. S., 11, 15, 30, 51n, 55, 57, 59, 61, 62, 66, 71, 72, 74, 92, 136

W

Walkerdine, V., 2n, 34, 132, 137
Watt, J., 48, 137
Wearne, D., 39, 133
Wenger, E., 66, 134
Wertsch, J. V., 32, 42, 43n, 66, 72, 137
Wittgenstein, L., 67, 70, 79, 137
Wolfe, M., 35, 135
Wood, G., 81, 137

Z

Zelizer, V. A., 24, 25, 137

Subject Index

◆ ◆ ◆

A

Abnormality, humanizing of, 37
Abstracting, human capacities for, 46
Abstraction, development as, 25
Abuse, 1, 78
    prevention, 12
Acting, play and, 73
Activistic inseparibility, 58
Activity-based method, 52
Activity theory, 43
Actor, as model performer, 73
Adaptation, 37
Adult, learning from, 100
Adult–child dyad, in Golden Key Project,
    91
Adulthood, 25
Affect, 98
After-school programs, 11
    Performance of a Young Lifetime,
    79, 79n
    Pregnant Productions, 79
Age-mixing
    at Sudbury Valley School, 100
Age-mixing, in Golden Key Project, 87,
    88–89, 90, 91
All Stars Talent Show Network, 12,
    77–79, 83, 94
Almanac of Education Choices (Mintz), 7
Alternative schools, 81
    Barbara Taylor School, 107–126, *see
    also* Barbara Taylor School

Project Golden Key, 83–93, *see also*
    Golden Key Project
    Sudbury Valley School Model,
    93–106, *see also* Sudbury Valley
    School
Alternative schools movement, 81
Analytic philosophy, 67
Ancient Greeks, conceptions of human ca-
    pacity for self-consciousness and ab-
    stracting, 46
Animal ancestors, continuity of, 25
Anti-institution, 11
Anti-violence programs for inner-city
    youth, All Stars Talent Show Net-
    work, 77–79
Appraisal, methods of, 12
Aptitudes, identifying of, 96
Aquinas, T., 47
Ariès, P., view on childhood, 21–22
Aristotle, view of world, 46–47
Army mental testing project, 36
"As if" position, 33

B

Babble, 124
Barbara Taylor School, 3, 5, 12, 102n, 127
    characteristics of developmental
    learning in, 114–119
    flow of potentially developmental
    activity, 119–122

history of, 111–114
  knowing and growth and, 126
  performance, play and
  improvisation at, 107–111
  relating to children as learners in,
  122–126
Behavior, 41
  classification of, 65
Behavioral change, 76
Behavioral laws, 37
Behaviorism, 37
  practical application of, 26–27
"Being ahead of yourself" activity, 74
Bias, of developmental psychology, 34–35
  schools as perpetuators of, 8
Biographical Sketch of an Infant, A (Dar-
  win), 20–21
Bloom, L., 8
Body movements, synchronization of, 32
Bullying, 1
Bureaucracy, educational, 17
Burman, E., issues with Kaye, 34

C

Care, educational model based on, 128
Castillo International, 12
Castillo Theatre, 12, 77, 79n
Causality, fundamentality of, 70
Causation, 35
Center for Developmental Learning, 77
Centuries of Childhood (Ari[sc155]s), 21
Change, Vygotsky's conception of, 57
Character traits, development of, 97
Charter schools, 81
CHAT, *See* Cultural historical activity the-
  ory
Child
  as active and constructive, 27–30
  coming-to-be-a-speaker, 61
  construction of, 20–25
  developing, discovery of, 40
  individual needs of, 40
  as measurable and adaptive, 25–27
  passive, 27
  psychological conception of, 24
  scientific conception of, 23
  as social and related, 31–35
  social construction of, 28
Child-centered approach to education, 40
Child study, historical perspective, 22–23

Childhood
  construction of, 20–25
  as cultural phenomenon, 21
  facts and memories of, 65
  views on, historical perspective,
  21–22
Christianity, recreation of, 47
Civilization, future, 25
Classification, 65
Cognition, 46, 98
  human, 39
  Piaget's insights into, 27
Cognitive activity, Vygotsky's view of, 43
Cognitive development, school task of, 39
Cognitive process, human, glorification of,
  45
Cognitive psychology, as ecologic invalid, 9
"Cognitive revolution," 35
Cognitive science, 37
Cole, M., 8
Collectively distributed activity, participa-
  tion in, in Golden Key Project, 90
Collectivism, 02
College enrollment, 18
Commercialism of society, 25
Commitment, 11–12
Community, 43
Community group, social therapy centers
  for, 76
Completion, Vygotsky's view on, 59
Concepts, 99
Concern, educational model based on, 128
Concrete operational child, 29
Connection, educational model based on,
  128
Consciousness, 42
Constructivism, 39
Continuing education center, Center for
  Developmental Learning and East
  Side Institute for Short Term Psy-
  chotherapy, 77
Correspondence, fundamentality of, 70
Courses, at Sudbury Valley School, 98
Creativity, intersubjective, 32
Cultural historical activity theory
  (CHAT), proponents of, 42
Cultural tools, appropriation of, 42
Cure, therapeutic, Wittgenstein's method
  of, 68
Curriculum
  cultural elitism of, 17
  in Golden Key Project, 91

D

Darwin, C., interest in children, 20–21
Data analysis, method of, 8
Data gathering, 22
Date, aggregating of, 36
Davydov, V. V., view on activities for stages
  of development, 72
Democratic institutions, transforming
  schools into, 127
Destructive model, hypothetic, 29
Developed form, preexistence of, 61
Development
  as approach to psychology, 22
  characteristics of, 2
  concern with, reasons for, 15–19
  creation of, 64
    in All Stars Talent Show
    Network, 78
    stages, 73
  evolutionary view of, 23
  form of, life event as, 88
  Golden Key project view of, 3
  holistic, 84
  learning/instruction and, 51, 56, 57,
  58–59, 62, 64
  meaning of, 73
  modern conception of, 2
  Piaget's stages of, 56
  psychology's myth of, 76
  reality of, 2
  revolutionary view of, 23
  separatist view on, 55
  as social-cultural, relational activity,
  15
  stages of, leading activities
  corresponding to, 72
Development community, developing, 65,
  66, 75
  further development of, 71
Development projects, 75
Developmental activity, 1
  conception of, 14
  learning severed from, 17
Developmental environment, creating of,
  12, 124
Developmental learning, at Barbara Taylor
  School, 125, 126
Developmental learning environments, creating of, 14
Developmental level
  grouping of children by, 100

  learning and, 15
Developmental needs, meeting of, defi-
  ciency in, 16
Developmental psychology
  as distinct branch of psychology,
  20–35
  distinguished from other branches
  of psychology, 20
  epistemology, 21
  historical perspective, 27
  status of, 27
Developmental theory and research
  antidevelopment of, 3
  learning theory and, 2
  problems with, 1–2, 2n
Diagnosis, refusal of, 12
Dialectical unity, 58, 59, 62
Discourse, creating of, 124
Discussions, academically oriented, 76n
Drama, in educational approach, 88
Dualistic science, Vygotsky's rejection of,
  51

E

East Side Institute for Short Term Psychotherapy, 12, 77
Economic value of children, 24
Economy, 16
Education
  banking system of, 41
  conceptions associated with, 5
  developmentally appropriate, 39–40
  information and skill-oriented
  system of, 15
  philosophical structure of, 5, 6
  psychological and philosophical
  roots of, ix
  traditional breakdown of, 86
Educational crisis, 14
  requirements of, 6–7
Educational models, current, 1–4
Educational practices
  ignoring of, 7
  standard, 15
Efficiency, needs for, 26
Egocentrism, childhood, 29–30
Elders, interaction with, 33–34
Elementary children laboratory, 75–76
  All Stars Talent Show Network,
  77–79

Center for Developmental Learning
and the East Side Institute for Short
Term Psychotherapy, 77
Performance of a Young Lifetime,
79, 79n
Pregnant Productions, 79
social therapy centers, 76–77
Elkonin, D., view on activities for stages of
development, 72
Emergent abilities, in Golden Key Project,
89
Emotional forms of life, new, creating of, 76
Emotional problems and pain, social ther-
apy centers for, 76–77
Emotionally disturbed (ED) students, 18
Empire State College, 14
End of Knowing: A New Developmental Way
of Learning, The (Newman &
Holzman), 13
Environment, see also specific type of envi-
ronment
interaction with, 61
orienting to, in Golden Key Project,
89
total, 61
Epistomological paradigm, adaptation by
social sciences, 47
Essences, fundamentality of, 70
Ethnography, 8
European aristocracy, relating to children,
21–22
Event, see also Life events
defined, 87–88, 88n
Evolution, 23
Evolutional process, presumption of, 21
Existing paradigms, challenging of, 7
Explanation, 65
Exploitation of children, economic, 24
Extra-commercial place, of children, 25

F

Family, good, features of, Golden Key Pro-
ject based on, 87
Family members, involvement in Golden
Key Project, 86, 90
Financial independence, 11
Forbes, D., 83
Formal operations stage of development, 29
Freud, S.
concept of ego, 29

individuated subject, 28
Freudian theory, incorporation into psychological theorizing, 24

G

Games, see also Language-game
playing of, 74
Gergen, K. J., 49
Goals 2000, see National Education Goals
Panel
Golden Key Project, 3, 83–84, 127
age ranges of children in, 86
boundaries in, 02
developmental education model of,
84–87
key characteristics of, 87
dialectic of creating a ZPD, 87–92
goal of, 85–86
learning subject and subject of
learning in, 90–92
organizing principle of, 90
Greenberg, D.
four acceptions of accepted view of
learning, 96
learning through theory
construction and, 95–96
views
on age-mixing, 100
on children's play, 99
on postindustrial era, 99
Group activities, life events organizing, 88
Group identity, 49
Growth
at Sudbury Valley School, 102–106
Vygotsky's view on, 60–61

H

Hall, G. S., as father of developmental psy-
chology, 22
Handicapped students, 18
High school completion rate, 18
History, study of, in Golden Key Project, 89
Homelessness, 16
Homeschooling, 81
Human experience, continuous, 46
Human functioning, processes of, 46
Human species, historical development of,
42

I

Identity, 35, 49
  formation of, 2
Identity politics, 18, 18n
Identity psychology, 49
Imitative activity, 43
Independence, practice of, 11
Individual, 96
  concept of, 46
Individualism, 35
  in Golden Key Project, 02
Industrialization, urban, 24
Inequality, reproduction and perpetuation of, 17–18
Infant, as biological organism, 32
Information processing theories, 37
Inner-city youth, community-based cultural organization for, 12
Inquiry, 52
Institutional arrangements, challenging of, 9
Institutional independence, 11
Instruction, *see also* Learning/instruction
  Vygotsky's view on, 57
Instrumentalism, 26
Intellectual development, invariant and linear stages of, 28
Intelligence, 37
  development of, 28, 29
Intention, in infant and children, 33
Intentionality, mutual, 32
Internal process, development of, 55–56
Interpretation, 65
Intersubjectivity, 32
Intrapsychic awareness, 76
Investigation, object of, 51

J

Joint activity, 62
  concepts of, 32, 33

K

Kantian categories of knowledge, 28
Kaye, K., Burman's view on, 34
"Knowers," production of, ix
Knowing, 5, 6, 35, 65
  development of, 28

developmental activity and, 74
growth and, 126
at Sudbury Valley School, 97–102, 102n
Knowing emotionally, 66
Knowing paradigm, human subjectivity and, 65
Knowledge
  construction of, 39, 40
  learning and, ix
  limits of, 6
  modern conception of, 48
  practicing method and, 52
Knowledge-based conception of learning, 96
Koffka, F., Vygotsky's criticism of, 57
Kratsov, G., 83, 85, 89
Kratsova, E., 83, 85, 89

L

Labor activity, 43
Laboratory experimentation, 36
Laboratory of Comparative Human Cognition, 8, 14
Language
  as activity, 74
  developed, starting point of, 61, 61n
  distinguishing of behavioral use and activity, 66
  play with, 74
  rules of, 75
  as social–cultural activity, 66
  thought and, 68
  understanding of, 69
  Vygotsky's view on, 66
  Wittgenstein's view on, 66–67, 68
Language activity, 66
Language-game
  as activity, 68
  playing of, 70
  value of, 69
  Wittgenstein's view on, 68–71
  ZPD-creating, 62
Learner
  conceptions of, 40, 41
  relating to children as, in Barbara Taylor School, 122–126
Learning
  acquisitional model of, 17
  approach to, for middle childhood and adulthood, 75

children compared with adults, 74
concern with, 15
crisis in, 14
development and, 51, 55, 56, 62, 64
developmental, 1
  history of, 3
general laws of, 37
Golden Key Project view of, 3, 87
good, Vygotsky's view on, 15
Greenberg's view, 96
hierarchical arrangements of,
  deconstruction of, 11
human, value of, 73
knowledge and, ix
Piaget's view, 37–38
psychology's conception of, 37
as quantifiable and measurable
  behavior of individual, 37
as social-cultural, relational activity,
  15
at Sudbury Valley School, 95–97
Vygotsky's view of, 43, 74
Learning activity
  concept of, in Golden Key Project,
    90–91
  structuring of, in Golden Key
    Project, 88
Learning capacity, 36
Learning crisis, increase in, 18
Learning disabled (LD) students, 18
Learning environment, organizing of, in
  Golden Key Project, 89
Learning/instruction
  development and, 56, 57, 58–59
    zone of proximal development
      and, 59–63
  separatist view on, 55
Learning/instruction–leading–develop-
  ment, development of, 58
Learning–leading–development, 91
Learning–leading–development–environ-
  ments of early childhood, 75
Learning outcomes, in Golden Key Project,
  92
Learning relationship, building of, with
  adult, 90
Learning theory, developmental theory
  and, 2
Legacy of Trust: Life After Sudbury Valley
  School Experience (Greenberg &
  Sadofsky), 102

Lev Vygotsky: Revolutionary Scientist (New-
  man & Holzman), 13, 14
Lewis, P., 83
Libertarian philosophy, Sudbury Valley
  School based on, 3, see also Sudbury
  Valley school
Life activity, 2
Life events, Golden Key Project centered
  around, 87–88, 88n
Life space, ZPD as, 60
Linguistic ZPD, 62
Linguistics, 8
Longitudinal approach to research, 8

M

Magnet schools, 81
"Making Meaning," 74–75
Manhattan therapy center, 77
Marx, K.
  dialectical historical materialism,
    Vygotsky's conception of, 57
  role in developing development
    community, 13
Marxist theorician, Vygotsky as, 53
"Math talk," creating an environment for,
  in Barbara Taylor School, 122–124
Mathematicians, children performing as,
  124
Mathematics achievement, 18
Meaning
  construction of, 48
  identification of, 69
  making of, in ZPD, 74–75
  understanding of, 69
  Wittgenstein's view on, 70
Meaning-making, 66, 124
Measurement, methods of, need for, 26
Medicalization, increasing of, 16
Memory, 39, 46
Mental acts, private, presumption of, 41
Mental health, 37
Mental hygiene movement, support of, 35
Mental operations, hypothetical, 39
Mental processes, individual, under-
  standing of, 60
Mental representation, rules of, 39
Mentalism, 35
Metacognition, 39
Metaphysical duality, 59

Metapsychology, 52
Method, methodology
   learning of, 97
   ongoing search for, 64
   practicing of, 11
   Vygotsky's conception of, 51–59
Mind, 41
   "in" society, 41–43
   individual, 96
Mind in Society (Vygotsky), 54, 55n
Model-building, 99
Modern epistemology, 5
Modernism, defined, 6
Mother, 61
Mother–child, joint construction of, 34
Mother–child dyad, analysis of, 32–33
Motives, in infant and children, 33
Multifamily groups, social therapy centers
      for, 76

N

National Education Goals Panel (Goals
      2000), 97
   Educate America Act, 18
National Education Goals Report, 18
Natural, conception of, 23
Natural science, 47
New England Association of Schools and
      Colleges, 95
New York City public schools, learning cri-
      sis in, 18
New York Institute for Social Therapy and
      Research, 10, 11
New York State Board of Regents, 77
Newman, F.
   movement to create independent
      institution, 9–10
   Sudbury Valley School and, 102,
      102n
19th century, education in, 16–17
Nondevelopmental schooling, 15–16
Nonepistemological environment, creating
      of, 129
Normal, conception of, 23
Number series problem, solving of, 70

O

Object
   infant's concept of, 28
   permanence, 29
Objectivity, doubts about, 65
Observational approach to research, 8
Ontology, 46
Options, new, creating of, 78
"Outer world," 31–32

P

Particular, 47
   notion of, 46
   Vygotsky's rejection of, 58
Particularity, notion of, 61
Passivity, child, 30–31
Past, educational policy of, 15
Pedagogical process, changing of, 86
Pedagogical tasks, solving of, 87
Pedagogy
   constructivist, 39
   rejection or negation of, 101–102
   transition to, 84
Perception, 46
Performance of a Young Lifetime, 79, 79n
Performative approach to education, bene-
      fits of, 128–129
Performers, human species as, 73
Performing
   capacity for, 73
   after childhood, 75
   development, talking and use of
      language by, 74
   play and, 73
Philosophical Investigations (Wittgenstein),
      67
Piaget, J.
   active child, 30–31
   asocial child, 32
   conception of child, 27–28
   continuation of legacy, 28
   developmental psychology, 27
   infant, 32
   paradigm and cognitive psychology,
      18
   theories on learning, 37–38
   "three mountain" task, 29
   view on thinking, 29
   Vygotsky's criticism of, 30–31, 32, 56
Pineau, E. L., view on performative ap-
      proach to education, 129
Pinocchio (Tolstoy), 85

Play
    free, 71–72
    at Sudbury Valley School, 99
    as and in the ZPD, 71–73
Play-acting, 72
Point of origin, 61
Policy, educational, 17
Postindustrial society, shift to, 99
"Postmodern" schools, creation of, 3
Postmodernism
    characteristics of, 6
    defined, 6
Practice
    community of, 65
    Vygotsky's view, 52
Practicing method, 52
Pregnancy, teen, prevention, 12
Pregnant Productions, 79
Pricing the Priceless Child (Ziegler), 24
Problem solving, 39, 76
    Greenberg's view on, 97
Problem-solving skills, development of, 40
Progress, Vygotsky's conception of, 57
Psychological functions, internalization of,
    42–43
Psychological investigation, earliest, 36
Psychological objects, new, 32, 37
Psychologist
    earliest interventions of, 35
    Vygotsky as, 52
Psychology
    conception of human development,
    2
    history of, 26
    task of, Vygotsky's view, 62
Public alternative schools, 81
Puzzle-copying task, 32

Q

Quantification, dominance of, 26
Questioning activity, in language games, 70

R

Race
    college enrollment and, 18
    school access and school success
    and, 17–18
Rationalism, philosophical, 23
Reality, 65

Recapitulatory needs, matching of, 22
Reductionism, 46
    biological and behaviorist, 23
    dominance of, 26
Reductionist science, Vygotsky's rejection
    of, 51, 58
Reflexes, conditional, 56
Relatedness, 32
Remarks on the Philosophy of Psychology
    (Wittgenstein), 70
Research
    developmental, reasons for, 21
    new methodology, 8
    psychological, historical perspective,
    36
Revolution, 23
Rockefeller University Lab, 9, 10
Roles
    acting out of, 72
    expected, 78
Russia
    educational systems in, Vygotsky
    and, 85
    experiment in development
    education, *see* Golden Key Project
Russian Academies of Education and of
    Sciences, 83
Russian schooling, Golden Key project
    and, *see* Golden Key project
Russian schools, causes of problems in, 91

S

School
    alternative to, 81, *see also*
    Alternative schools
    mismanagement, 6
"School dumb," 14
School failure, root of, 6
School setting, social interaction within, 41
"School smart," 14
Schooling, 99
Schooling the Poor, 16–17
Schools for growth
    arguments against, 16
    key elements of, 1
Science activity, Vygotsky's view on, 51
"Scientific mind," 23
Scientific psychology
    changes occurring in, 18
    current education models misguided
    by, 1–4

Seasons, change of, 88
Self
    emergence of, 2
    future, 25
Self-consciousness, human capacities for,
    46
Self-criticism, 11
Self-evaluation, at Sudbury Valley School,
    102
Semiotic mechanisms, 33
Sentimental value of children, 24, 25
Separatists, view on development, 55
Skinner, B. F., behaviorism and, 26
Social constructionism, 47–50
Social–cultural activity
    language as, 66
    speaking/thinking as, 66
Social development, 43
Social epistomology, 5
Social etiquette, learning of, 97
Social interaction, 32, 41
    child's adaptation to, 32
    importance of, 32
Social sciences, 47
Social system, 34
Social therapy centers, 12, 76–77
    activities of, 77
Sociality, predisposition to, 32
Society, 61
Speaking, activity of, 66–71
Speaking/thinking, as social cultural activ-
    ity, 66
Speech
    developed, 62
    egocentric, 29
    rudimentary, 62
    shaping and reshaping of, 62
Stalinist repression, Vygotsky as victim of,
    54
Standard of living, 16
    rise in, 24
State, contractual relationship with, 11
Status quo, 17
    preservation of, 34
Students
    grading or sorting of, 12
    tracking of, 40, 96
Study, object of, creation of, 64
Subjectivity, human, 65–66
Subject
    in Golden Key Project, 91
    at Sudbury Valley School, 98

Sudbury Valley School, 93–94, 127
    beliefs, 94
    growing at, 102–106
    knowing at, 97–102, 102n
    language of, 101
    learning at, 95–97
    philosophy of, 3
    student body of, 94–95
Symptoms, controlling of, 16

T

Teacher, discontent, 6
"Theories of the mind," reintroduction of,
    18
Theory construction, process of learning
    through, 95–96
Therapeutic modality, Nonepistemologi-
    cal, 65
Thinking
    child's, development of, 56
    independent, development of, 40
    logical, 29
    proper, 47
Thinking and Speech (Vygotsky), 54
Third World Psychologists, 02
Thorndike, E., view on development, Vy-
    gotsky's rejection of, 56
Thought
    egocentric, 29
    language and, 68
    Vygotsky's view on, 66
    Western modes of, 2
    word and, 66
"Three mountain" task, 29
Time, study of, in Golden Key Project, 89
Tolstoy, L., 85
Tool-and-result methodology, 52, 64, 65,
    128
    dialectical unity of, 52
    language and, 66
    search for, 58
    ZPD and, 60
Tool-and-retoolish method, play as, 72
Tool use, 43
Totalities, 57
Totality, individual-and-society, 61
Tracking, 40, 96
Tractatus Logic-Philosophicus (Wittgen-
    stein), 67
Traditional method, 52
Training, 37

Trauma, psychic, 28
Turn taking, 32

U

Understanding
    development of, 40
    therapeutic, 65–66
    understanding of, 67
Unscientific Psychology: A Cultural–Performatory Approach to Understanding Human Life (Newman & Holzman), 13

V

Verbal Behavior (Skinner), 27
Violence, 16
    approach to, in All Stars Talent Show Network, 78
Vygodskaya, G., 83
Vygotskian development projects, 84
Vygotsky, L. S., 10
    activity theory, 43
    analysis of play, 72
    biographical information on, 53–54
    challenge to evolutionary view of development, 23
    conception of methodology, 51–59
    concern with learning and development, 54–55
    contemporary followers of, 52
    criticism of Piaget, 56
    Golden Key Project and, 86
    methodological breakthrough of, 13
    rejection of Piaget's views, 30–31
    sense of play, with language, 74
    tool-and-result methodology, *see* Tool-and-result methodology
    views
    on community of practice, 65
    on consciousness, 42
    on development, 85
    on free play, 71–72
    on internalization of psychological functions, 42–43
    on performing, 73
    works of, 54
    zone of proximal development and, 43, *see* Zone of proximal development

W

War on Poverty, 18
Watson, J., behaviorism and, 26
Wittgenstein, L.
    language-game and, 68–71
    methodological breakthrough of, 13
    views on language, 66–67 , 67n, 68
"Woman way of knowing," 5
Word
    meaning of, 69
    thought and, 66
Writing, child's readiness to learn, 55–56

Y

Young children, as model performers, 73

Z

Zone of proximal development (ZPD), 43, 59–63, 71, 74
    All Stars Talent Show Network, 78
    dialectic of creating, 87–92
    in Golden Key Project, 91
    of infancy and early childhood, 74
    linguistic, 62
    overlapping, 100, 101
    performatory, 75
    play as and in, 71–73
    shaping of, 75